How I Became a
TERRORIST

Edan Ganie
w/ Cassandra Woody

How I Became a
TERRORIST

Islamophobia and the
Oppressive Aftermath of
9-11 on the Muslim Community

TATE PUBLISHING
AND ENTERPRISES, LLC

How I Became a Terrorist
Copyright © 2013 by Edan Ganie. All rights reserved.

No part of this publication may be reproduced, stored in a retrieval system or transmitted in any way by any means, electronic, mechanical, photocopy, recording or otherwise without the prior permission of the author except as provided by USA copyright law.

The opinions expressed by the author are not necessarily those of Tate Publishing, LLC.

Published by Tate Publishing & Enterprises, LLC
127 E. Trade Center Terrace | Mustang, Oklahoma 73064 USA
1.888.361.9473 | www.tatepublishing.com

Tate Publishing is committed to excellence in the publishing industry. The company reflects the philosophy established by the founders, based on Psalm 68:11,
"The Lord gave the word and great was the company of those who published it."

Book design copyright © 2013 by Tate Publishing, LLC. All rights reserved.
Cover design by Junriel Boquecosa
Interior design by Honeylette Pino

Published in the United States of America

ISBN: 978-1-62746-789-6
1. Biography & Autobiography / Personal Memoirs
2. Social Science / Discrimination & Race Relations
13.10.29

When governments fear the people, there is liberty. When the people fear the government, there is tyranny.

—Thomas Jefferson

I would like to dedicate this book to my family, my wife and three children as well as my brothers, who have experienced the horrible interrogations and additional security searches at the airport, immigration services, and border crossings, which often require their patience for hours as they travelled with me.

I would like to thank my family members and office staff whose help were invaluable in the preparation and compilation of the book. I especially would like to thank Cassandra Woody who made it possible for me to complete this book.

CONTENTS

Chapter One: September 11, 2001:
A Day That Will Live on in Infamy 11

Chapter Two: The Trouble Really Begins 19

Chapter Three: My Family History 29

Chapter Four: Strife Breaks Out in Guyana 37

Chapter Five: Bare Foot School Days 41

Chapter Six: Coming to America 51

Chapter Seven: Making Cheese 61

Chapter Eight: Becoming an Entrepreneur 65

Chapter Nine: We have to Comply, Period 71

Chapter Ten: Profiling, TSA, and Secondary
Screening 83

Chapter Eleven: Prove Your Patriotism or Leave 95

Chapter Twelve: Are You Waiting for Me? 107

Chapter Thirteen: By Land and Air,
Harassment is There 113

Chapter Fourteen: More Money, More Problems .. 121

Chapter Fifteen: I Must Interrogate You but
I Don't Know What Questions to Ask 127

Chapter Sixteen: Terrorist, Terrorist supporter,
or terrorist sympathizer 137

Chapter Seventeen: Are You a Terrorist? 157

Epilogue 163

CHAPTER ONE:

September 11, 2001: A Day That Will Live on in Infamy

It was about 6:00 a.m. Pacific Time on the morning of September 11, 2001. I was at the mosque offering my ritual pre-dawn prayers and then I returned home. I sat down with my morning cup of coffee, turned on the television and saw the news that a plane had flown into one of the twin towers of the World Trade Center.

The visions I saw flashing across my television that day I will never forget as long as I live. I knew right then that the world would be changed forever, but I had no idea yet that my life at a very personal level would be also. As I sat in my living room, eyes glued to the TV, I fell into complete shock and I knew the rest of the country was likely doing the same. We were united in grief and disbelief that the horrifying situation being broadcast live on the news was really happening.

Almost as ritualistic as my morning prayers was the time I spent watching the NBC morning news with my wife as we welcomed the day together with a cup of coffee and spent some quality time chatting, just the two of us before the kids were up. That particular day I called out to my wife the moment I turned the news

Edan Ganie

on so she too could witness the tragic event that was unfolding before me. She rushed into the living room.

"What is it?" she asked.

"Look at this," I said without taking my eyes off the shattered New York skyline on the screen.

"Oh my," she said, putting a hand over her mouth as she dropped down on the couch next to me. "What is happening? What is this?"

"It was a plane," I explained. "Somehow a plane just crashed right into it."

"A plane?" my wife asked confused. "How did a plane crash into a building like that?"

Before I could answer my wife, a second plane flew into the second tower.

"What is going on?" my wife said again. "What is happening?"

"I have no idea," I said as I tried to absorb the second shock of watching yet another plane smash into the side of the second tower.

My wife and I stayed fixed in our places in front of the television for some time. We listened intently to one reporter after the next cover the tragedy, waiting for an answer as to how not one, but two planes somehow fell off course so badly that they flew right into two prominent fixtures in the New York cityscape. None of it made any sense at all.

I am Guyanese and migrated to the United States in 1978. I have several friends and relatives who live in New York and New Jersey and work in Manhattan. I knew that a couple of fellow schoolmates actually worked in the trade center. Looking at a destroyed

How I Became a Terrorist

Manhattan in complete and utter chaos, I found myself not only mourning a great loss for the country, and even the entire world, but also fretting about the welfare of loved ones and acquaintances I knew many who may have been injured or even killed.

An hour or so after all this began, our children awoke and came to find their parents stunned on the sofa.

"What is going on?" one of my sons asked, standing beside the sofa starring at the horror on the TV.

"Two planes have hit the World Trade Center Towers," I answered. "It's horrible. It's absolutely horrible."

"How?" my daughter asked.

"They don't know much yet," I told her. "But it appears to be an attack."

I went on to try to give some kind of explanation for the horror that was taking place and explain that the country was under attack. I was having trouble myself understanding it all so it was difficult for me, but I did my best to let my children know what was happening over in New York, what was happening to the world.

As shaken as I was by the attacks, I knew that I had to pull myself together and get to work. By nine a.m. that morning I went into my office and began meeting with staff and going about my daily work. At around half past ten my secretary came into my office.

"Mr. Ganie," she said, "there is a gentleman here to see you out front but he won't say who he is."

"A gentleman?" I asked a little confused. I couldn't think of a meeting I had scheduled for the day and I wasn't expecting anyone. I pulled up my calendar and double-checked to be sure something hadn't slipped

13

Edan Ganie

my mind and saw that I was right; I hadn't made an oversight. There was nothing on my schedule for the day.

I pointed to my computer and held up a finger to let my secretary know that I was in the middle of something and that I needed some time to finish up. After I wrapped up what I was doing, I got up and went out to see who this mystery man was who needed to speak to me so badly he couldn't make an appointment.

"Hello," I said to the gentleman seated in the receptionist area. "My receptionist tells me you need to speak to me."

"Yes, Mr. Ganie," the man said. "My name is Ethan Wheelwright and I'm with the FBI."

I shook Officer Wheelwright's hand and asked him what I could do for him.

"Could we speak in your office?" he asked. "Privately."

"Okay," I said leading him into my office. I couldn't imagine what an FBI agent could want to speak with me privately about. The entire day seemed like a very strange dream, or better, a nightmare, between national tragedies and unexplained FBI agents showing up at my office.

"Have a seat," I said, gesturing to one of the chairs that sat facing my desk. "What can I do for you, Ethan? I must admit, I am a little confused"

"I'm a special agent with the FBI," he started. "And I have some questions I need you to answer."

"About what?" I asked.

"I'm interested to know why you were at the airport yesterday," the agent said, pulling out a recorder and a notepad.

How I Became a Terrorist

The reason I was at the airport started with a discussion I had with some friends at the mosque one day. We were discussing the Quibla (the direction to Mecca that Muslims around the world face when they pray), and I said that I would get my GPS so that we could confirm what direction we really should be facing. I had lent the GPS to an acquaintance of mine, though, so I met him at the local airport to get it back. This was on September 10, 2001.

You see, I am a pilot and I met a fly buddy named Tony at the airport to grab the GPS because he had borrowed it. I called Tony and asked him to meet me at the airport with the GPS. I wanted to confirm the direction of Mecca so I asked Tony to do it with me while we were at the airport. I didn't explain to Tony why I wanted to know the direction at the time, only that I was trying to figure out where it really was. Tony met me and helped me find the direction, and then we went on our ways.

The following day when the planes hit the towers, Tony remembered me and, not knowing me very well, he called the FBI. It seemed a strange coincidence that I was at an airport just the day before asking about Mecca, so he felt that he needed to report it to authorities. A Muslim pilot also set alarms off for him, which unfortunately would be the case from that point forward for any Muslim interested in flying a plane. Tony's call was the reason Wheelwright was there to see me, but I didn't know that at the time. All that he told me was that he knew I was at the airport and wanted to know why.

15

Edan Ganie

I agreed to continue the interview with the agent. I had nothing to hide and had done nothing wrong, so I figured that compliance would be the easiest way to resolve whatever it was that was going on.

He ended up questioning me about where I was born, how I got to the United States, about my family, my business, my friends, my travels, my reason for being at the airport with my GPS. You name it. He questioned me about everything that had ever happened from my birth to that very moment. Finally after an hour and a half of questioning, our meeting came to a close.

"Thank you for your cooperation, Mr. Ganie," he said as he got up to leave.

"Not a problem," I told him. I was glad that the interview was finally over.

Wheelwright left my office and I continued with my work. I went home and told my wife about my day and the FBI agent. Because Wheelwright hadn't told me the entire reason for his visit, I was still wondering why exactly he came to visit me. It was not until months after my interrogation that Tony came to my office and explained that he was the one who called the FBI. I wasn't upset with Tony for what he did, and I told him that. I could see how he was only trying to be cautious and I could also see how the entire incident could have triggered some alarms to him after watching the attacks and listening to unending news discussion of Muslim terrorists. It was also an unfortunate coincidence that we had met just the night before the 9-11 attacks and I needed the GPS but didn't say why. It was an ill-fated misunderstanding when all was said and done, but I

How I Became a Terrorist

didn't know just how ill-fated yet. That first encounter with the FBI was only the tip of the iceberg for me, which you will see later.

CHAPTER TWO:

The Trouble Really Begins

Two years went by after that interview with the FBI without incident. I didn't think much of it because I just assumed that, because I had explained myself and cleared up the misunderstanding, everything was fine. I was sorely mistaken.

On September 19, 2003, my brother and my nephew, who are of East Indian decent like myself, were all onboard Alaska Airlines Flight 16 from Seattle to Miami. I was going to Miami for a business meeting and my brother and nephew were going along for a weekend vacation.

At that time I was president of a healthcare company, which is located in Olympia, Washington. I had an Alaska Airlines "MVP" card and regularly purchased ten to fifteen flights per month for myself and the physicians I employed. I probably flew about 100,000 miles annually during that time. Because I had the MVP card and the miles helped my business, I bought the tickets for all three of us with my Alaska Airlines credit card.

The day of the trip we arrived at the airport, went through security, and got our boarding passes. We all

Edan Ganie

packed light enough that we didn't need to check any luggage. It was only going to be a two day trip, so we were able to get everything we needed in a carry-on. Anyone who travels often knows that if you can get away without having to check bags, your trip will be that much easier.

So, we got our boarding passes and waited for our plane to arrive. It came right on time and the three of us boarded and took our seats in Row 8; we were sitting together in seats D, E, and F. Not long after we had settled in, a flight attendant came over and leaned down to speak to my brother.

"I'm going to need you to come with me, sir," she said sternly. "I'm afraid that we can't allow you on this flight because you haven't paid for your ticket."

"I would like to come as well," I interjected. "I'm the one who purchased the tickets."

"That will be fine," she said to me.

We all three got up from our seats and exited the plane. For anyone who has never been escorted off a plane, it is not a pleasant experience, especially for a Muslim of Indian decent post-9-11. I didn't notice if any of the passengers took notice of what was happening, but in my mind I could imagine what some of them must have been thinking, watching three men who looked like they were from the East being taken off the plane, and it turned my stomach.

When we got to the boarding station, the woman who was working the boarding desk explained that the address for the credit card used to purchase my brother's ticket did not match his address.

How I Became a Terrorist

"Yes, that is because I purchased the ticket for my brother," I explained again.

"I see," the woman said from behind her desk. "Go ahead and board them," she told the flight attendant, and then added, "I apologize for the misunderstanding."

We boarded the plane for the second time and I decided to get a book I had brought along, so I stood up and opened the overhead compartment to get into my bag. As I wrestled my carry-on out from between my brother's and nephew's bags, I decided I'd just put my piece of luggage in the overhead bin across the aisle so I wouldn't have to cram it back in the crowded bin.

I grabbed my book, zipped my tiny suitcase up again, and then turned to the bin across the aisle and placed my bag there in a nearly empty compartment. I sat back down and began to read my book, but was interrupted by a flight attendant.

"Excuse me, sir," she said, leaning down so that her face was level with mine. "Where is your carry-on?

I looked up from my book and pointed to the place I had just put my bag. She nodded, and without a word she walked away. I returned to reading my book while my brother and nephew dozed off as we waited for takeoff.

Only a few minutes later I looked up to see the captain standing at the cockpit door with the Port of Seattle police. They were accompanied by the flight attendant who had asked me about my bag and the Alaska Airlines ground crew supervisor.

Edan Ganie

The police officers came straight to us and one said, "The three of you, take your bags and get off the plane. You're not going on this flight."

We were all stunned by the demand, but we didn't say a word in response. We quickly and quietly gathered our belongings and exited the plane for a second time, perplexed by the curtness of the officer and the fact that we were being kicked off a flight for no reason at all.

Once off the plane, the Port of Seattle officers separated us and asked for identification, which we provided. Each of us did exactly as we were told. We just wanted to get on with the day and get back on our flight, so we cooperated every step of the way. My brother and nephew were asked by the officer where they were flying from.

"From here," my nephew stated. "We're residents. We're going to Florida for a quick vacation."

The officers seemed surprised when my nephew said he lived in Washington and that he hadn't flown in from another city.

"What is this about?" I asked the officer who had detained me, a stocky middle-aged guy named Fred Harper with slicked back hair and a goatee. "Why were we forced off the flight?"

"We have the right to remove you from the plane," Harper answered as he planted both his huge feet to the ground and crossed his arms over his chest.

"I don't want to hear what *you* have to say," I said to the beefy officer who had made it a point to let me know he didn't like me since the whole thing started. Fred didn't take my response very well. He was obviously

How I Became a Terrorist

not as good at taking insults as he was at throwing them around.

"Get out of my airport!" he spat as flashed red. "Get outta here now or I'm going to take you upstairs!"

I had no idea what "taking me upstairs" meant, but I gathered that it wasn't something I wanted to do.

A man who was waiting to board another flight happened to notice Harper's tirade and he came over to speak to my brother, nephew, and me, and the police about what was going on.

"My name is Devon Cunningham," he said as he approached us. "I've just witnessed all this and I wanted to come over to see what's going on here."

Devon turned to the policeman and asked, "What is the problem here? This looks pretty sketchy from where I'm sitting."

"We're handling it," one of the officers said. "This doesn't involve you."

Devon turned back to the three of us and said, "Can I do anything for you all? It doesn't look like you're being treated fairly."

I explained to the kind-hearted stranger what had happened, but assured him we would get it worked out. I then thanked him for his concern and told him he'd better get to his flight. He asked if we were sure he couldn't help and I insisted we would be fine.

We were kept at the gate area for over an hour. During that time, two different TSA representatives came over to ask us yet again for our identification, which we had already showed everyone at the beginning of the ordeal. We were kept separated from each other

Edan Ganie

the entire time, and not once did someone say what all this was about.

Devon wasn't the only person concerned about how we were being treated through all this. There was an officer named Cameron who floated around among the three of us through all the questioning and waiting. He repeatedly apologized to all of us.

"I'm Japanese," he said to my nephew. "I'm from Hawaii originally. The way you all are being treated since 9-11 is terrible."

My nephew just nodded his head so Cameron continued.

"It was the same way for our people after Pearl Harbor. People treat you like you're less than human because the way you look. It's not fair. People make you into a villain. Every Muslim is a terrorist in their eyes just like anyone who had Japanese blood bombed Pearl Harbor. It's awful."

Cameron was absolutely right. A small group commits a crime against humanity and millions of innocent people pay the price. After Pearl Harbor, anyone who even looked Japanese was the enemy, no matter where they were from or how much they disagreed with Japan's actions. An entire race was labeled evil for the acts of a corrupt government. Japanese who fled Japan in hopes of escaping such a government were suddenly lumped in with evil-doers. Men and women proud of the fact they were first, second, or third generation Americans were suddenly stripped of their American identity by people who

How I Became a Terrorist

hated them for their ethnicity and who used patriotism as grounds for that hate.

September 11, 2001, was also a day that will live on in infamy, and it was a day, just like Pearl Harbor, that left a deep scar on history and on the American people. Along with stealing the lives away from almost 3,000 people, the terrorists stole the identity of peaceful Muslims around the world. 9-11 ushered in a new brand of fear, racism and hate for anyone who wore a turban or bowed to Mecca. And people everywhere perpetuate the stigmas that are stealing civil rights from Muslim-Americans today. I was learning that lesson firsthand as I sat in the SeaTac Airport and handed over my ID to one agent after the next who looked at me as if I were a terrorist myself.

When the TSA agents came back with our identification cards, one of them said, "It wasn't our decision to remove you from the plane. This is all just a big misunderstanding."

I'd say it was. And the only explanation we were given was that the flight crew "didn't feel comfortable having you on the flight."

When it was all finally over, the Alaska Airline Supervisor, Larry Williams, told us that the airline had no more flights to Miami that day.

"We apologize for the inconvenience," he said. "And we will be refunding the money for your tickets."

I told the officers that I wanted to check the other airlines to see if perhaps there was another flight going to Miami. At this, Officer Cameron insisted that we

Edan Ganie

leave the airport per Officer Harper's instructions. He then escorted us out of the airport.

Although there are some who would have people that look like me banned from flights for irrational fear of "what we might do," there are still plenty of people out there who realize the injustice of racial profiling. I saw that in Devon that day. I also realized that when a local television news crew showed up to interview us about the incident. The episode had been an inconvenience at best and a grave injustice at worst, but I was relieved to see that there were people who were as offended as I was about the event.

Along with interviewing the three of us, the station also interviewed a passenger named Abe on Flight 16 as the flight arrived in Miami.

"Do you think the airport authorities were justified in their actions?" the reporter asked.

"No, I don't," Abe answered. "They didn't look threatening at all. They were quiet, and there was zero resistance when they were asked to leave the plane."

Abe, who explained he worked for Microsoft in Redmond, Washington, sat three rows behind us on the plane. In an interview not on camera, he said that we were waiting quietly for the plane to take off like all the other passengers and he didn't see us do anything to cause concern. According to the news program, an unidentified spokesman for the airport security claims that one of my companions pointed his finger like a gun at a flight attendant.

Nothing about anything we did that day could have been perceived by Alaska Airlines as threatening or

How I Became a Terrorist

disruptive to Flight 16 on September 19, 2003, and no one articulated any behavior that could have been seen as a risk to other passengers. We were quiet, compliant, and broke no laws or airport rules, and no one could ever tell us why it was we were singled out in the first place. I had a good idea what it was that put targets on each of us though, I just didn't want to believe it.

We filed a complaint against Alaska Airlines and Port of Seattle alleging discrimination. Over a two-year period there were a series of communications involving the United State Department of Transportation Federal Aviation Administration, Alaska Airlines, and the American Civil Liberties Union (ACLU). My attorney and I met with representatives from the Department of Transportation and the Federal Aviation Administration, and after some negotiations we identified three areas where action needed to be taken: 1) Port leadership needed to see that Officer Harper was a problem; 2) there needed to be understanding of the different cultures that used the airport; and 3) more education and customer training was needed.

In April of 2005 I received communication, through my attorney, from the Federal Aviation Administration after they concluded their investigation. It turned out that Officer Harper was retired from the Port of Seattle. I found this interesting since he looked to be in his early forties when I met him.

We were told that the Port of Seattle agreed to collaborate with the "Hate Free Zone" to provide diversity training to Port of Seattle Officers and that all officers would receive training. Also, Port of Seattle

Edan Ganie

would develop internal procedures to ensure that the Port Coordinator would be notified of complaints based on race, color, national origin, sex, creed or disability and those complaints would be provided to the FAA within fifteen days of receipt.

I continue to travel frequently using SeaTac airport, but Alaska Airlines is certainly not my airline of choice these days. I have since switched to Delta Airlines for almost all of my travel. However I know though that it isn't just one airline that is the root of the problems I face. It is prejudice and profiling that are my true enemies. Local police, TSA employees, and Customs and Border Protection (CBP) officers, they don't see Edan Ganie; they see a would-be terrorist—a man who has been living in caves in the Middle east, plotting with Al Qaeda and planning destruction for the West. They see my complexion and hear my accent, and I immediately become a threat rather than who I really am: a father, a husband, a son, a brother, and an immigrant turned citizen who has loved and respected this country from the day I stepped foot on its soil.

The fact is, I came from very humble beginnings, and to me America was my shot at a life that my parents, grandparents, and so on only dreamed of. All those officers see is a boarding pass with the frightful "SSSS" across it, marking me a high risk passenger, but what they don't see is who I truly am. If they did, they would know that I would never dream of doing anything to hurt a country that has given me so much.

CHAPTER THREE:

My Family History

My ancestors are from India, but details beyond that are vague. Because the British kept such poor records of those they colonized, and also because plantation owners had a tendency to destroy documents belonging to laborers, it is very hard to get a complete picture of my family history. I do know a little about my family's roots, however. My parents, who were laborers themselves, had a few records of my ancestors in India. I was told that my grandparents on my father's side came from Punjab province and my mother's ancestors' origins were unknown.

How my family came to British Guiana (British Guiana gained it's independence from the British in 1964 and became Guyana) was this; the British West India Trading Company brought Indian laborers to work the sugar plantations in Guyana, just as they did to other countries around the globe. Once slavery was abolished, European settlements everywhere needed to replace slave labor somehow. For the British, Indians must have looked like a perfect solution, so at around the turn of the century the British started to seek out Indians to work on the plantations to do the work African slaves once did. They knew they'd have to be

Edan Ganie

clever about how they convinced Indians to go, and clever they certainly were.

British plantation owners promised Indians a better life and so Indians were lured into migrating to Guyana to do back-breaking work that never offered anything better than what was left behind in India. My family was included in the many that left India in search of a brighter future. My grandparents were among the last members of Indians lured by the British into travelling to the promised land of Guyana.

Like most peasants from India in those times, my grandparents worked and lived on the land of their landlords (who were called Zamindars) back home in India. These Zamindars controlled the villages and had enormous power over the peasants. The Zamindars gave peasants land to live and work on, and in return they would pay the landlords by giving them a percentage of their crops yielded from the land. They were never given the chance to own land though, so when the British showed up claiming that land ownership was a possibility, people were more than willing to load themselves onto boats and sail off to a better life.

The British weren't known for keeping their promises to Indians and this instance was no exception to that rule. This Promised Land they painted never existed. Indians were not trading in for better lives; they were merely being transplanted to do the exact same thing in a different country while the British reaped the benefits. Almost half of the Indians who set sail for a new life never even made it to Guyana to face the disappointment that awaited them. The

How I Became a Terrorist

poor conditions and lack of medical attention on ships resulted in countless deaths of Indians in route for Guyana.

Along with securing cheap labor, the British also had a little triangle scheme going that was a great benefit to them. They would set off from India with loads of servants, drop those who survived the trip off on the islands and pick up goods such as produce, spices, gold routed to England for delivery before they headed back to India for more laborers. It was ideal if you weren't on the side being exploited.

My grandparents and their families who came from India settled on the West Coast of Demerara, more precisely at Tushcen plantation.

Back in India, births were not recorded in the villages so it was hard to determine the ages of my grandparents when they arrived in Guyana, but we do know that they came to Guyana as indentured immigrants and were bound by contract to work with the British in the sugar plantations for a number of years. The males were bound for five years and women for three years in most cases. After their servitude was complete, the laborers were allowed to live on the land of the plantations and in most cases were given a small plot of land to live off.

I never saw or met any of my grandparents, as they were all deceased before I was even born, so everything I know about them has been passed down to me from my parents. Although I never knew them, I can only imagine the disillusionment they must have experienced once they arrived in Guyana. They believed they were going to make something of themselves. They believed

31

Edan Ganie

they had been offered a way out of hardship, only to land right back into it. Luckily though time was slowly bringing the family out of poverty—the operative word here being *slowly*.

My paternal grandmother, who I have been told was stunning, worked for a plantation manager who was from Scotland named Donald Ritchie. He was brought by the British plantation owners to manage the sugar estate on the Essequibo, which is the name of an area of Guyana. My grandmother became Ritchie's lover. Ritchie forged a relationship with my grandmother and they ended up with three sons and one daughter who were half Indian, half Scottish.

Ritchie eventually left Essequibo and returned to Scotland, leaving my grandmother and the children behind. My grandmother later married my grandfather, who was also Indian. They had two sons, my father, Abdul Ganie, and his brother. My father spent most of his youth working the rice fields with his half-brothers.

Because Guyana did not, as the British had claimed, offer any better a life, most Indians there didn't go to school past the age of twelve, if they went to school at all. My father was fortunate enough to have made it to what was the equivalent to junior high school.

My mother, Nazrul Bikhari, never stepped foot in a school building. My maternal grandfather died when my mother was just a child, so my mom had to help the family (there were six children total) rather than attend school. It was either eating or education, and an education does you no good if you starve to death, so she never even got to start school.

How I Became a Terrorist

My mother's first responsibility was to help take care of cattle. She would go with her mother in the mornings to help milk the cows and then take them to the pastures for grazing. Then at the end of the day my mother and her siblings would help my grandmother gather grass for the cows to eat during the night. My mother was only five years old when she started tending livestock with my grandmother and her siblings.

My grandmother would milk the cows every day and my mother, aunts and uncles would go around the village trying to sell the milk. The income from the cows would help to supplement the wages from my elder uncles, my mother's older brothers, who were in their early teens and had moved on to working on the sugar estate.

My mom started working in a plantation fulltime when she was only twelve years old, but my father, since he did get some education, didn't start until he was fifteen when he left the rice fields and school for the west coast of Guyana where the sugar plantations were.

While my father was working on the sugar cane estate, he and my uncle, along with the other Indians who were cane cutters, were able to convince the plantation owners to approach their work in a new way. Where the plantations owners had been dividing workers up into separate groups, each to perform a different task, my dad and his group suggested that those cutting the cane also fetch and load it into the punts for transport. Their new method resulted in three workers doing as much work as seven under the old African slave system the plantation owners once used.

33

Edan Ganie

In turn, the new system allowed hard working Indian laborers to earn better wages.

It was on the plantation working that my parents actually met. While my father was working as a "cane cutter," my mother worked serving water to the cane cutters. In accordance with India's customs, which do not permit any dating, my parents marriage was influenced by their elders and they were soon married.

My mother's older brother worked alongside my dad, so that is how it all took place. My dad began the conversation with my uncle, and then my uncle with my mother's family, and by the time my mom was fourteen and my dad twenty, the two were wed.

My parents worked the land like their parents had before them and they had nine children in the meantime, five boys and four girls. At first my parents and older siblings lived in what were called "logies," which were primitive living quarters that plantation owners built for laborers. They resembled long townhouses, but laborers and their families were given minimal space within them. Each family working on the plantation got a one bedroom unit with a small half wall dividing it; there was an area for cooking, and another small area for sleeping and living. This was standard for each family, despite its size. If you had three children or thirteen, you were given the same size living area.

My family was lucky in that after my parents had their fourth child, they obtained a home lot, which the plantation owners made available to certain categories of workers. My father also qualified for a loan that the plantation offered to build a house. He then built

How I Became a Terrorist

a small two bedroom house in the Tuschen housing village being developed at that time (this was in the fifties). The house my father built was the house I was born and raised in, so I never had to experience life in a logie.

My father was able to provide my family with their own home because of his relentless hard work. He was regarded as one of the best cane cutters on the plantation. He commanded a high degree of respect from his fellow plantation workers and even from the field managers on the plantation. I remember as a boy how other workers in the village would come to my father to help them with issues in the field. They would also seek my father's help with personal matters.

I was the seventh out of my parents' nine children, so I was one of the youngest. That proved beneficial for me in a number of ways. One, I never had to live in a logie, but most importantly because one of my older sisters completed her education and became a school teacher, so she was able to help us even if we weren't able to go to school.

Life in Guyana was never easy, per se, for my family, but we were fortunate in many ways. My father, although a laborer, was respected and able to build his own home. And we did get some education, which was more than many could say in the area. There was something that happened in Guyana, however, that made life difficult for everyone. By the time I was five, it seemed the country was completely dividing, and even crumbling.

CHAPTER FOUR:

Strife Breaks Out in Guyana

Because the part of Guyana in which my family lived was a British colony, we were feeling the aftermath of World War II, as Great Britain was having problems supporting its colonies, which meant that food and rations were often scarce.

The needs that stemmed from the effects of WWII acted as a springboard for a civil revolution referred to as the "80 Days" Strike that was organized by the British and American intelligence agencies. The strike seemed to cause more harm than anything else, though, as it was a contributor to violence and strife throughout the country.

On top of that, Guyana had its first and second prime minister elections. The People's Progressive Party (PPP), the first organized political party in Guyana, was formed by Dr. Cheddi Jagan, an admirer of Marx, along with his wife Janet Jagan, and Forbes Burnham. After the elections of 1955 and the party's less than stellar rule of the county that had been attempted by novices, there grew a rift in the leadership.

In the 1963 elections, Burnham formed his own party called the People's National Congress (PNC) aided by the CIA and the Queen's Counsel. The PNC

Edan Ganie

did not, however, win the elections, but it did collate with a third party, the D' Aguiar Party. This gave the collated party a majority rule and Burnham became the Prime Minister. The ethnic make up of Guyana at the time was predominantly African Black and Indian, with a minority of Portuguese who were predominantly business class shop owners, although they were originally brought to Guyana to work and build the railroad. There was also a fair amount of Amerindians, who were the native Indians that occupied the land prior to the European coming there.

The 1964 "80 Days" Strike was also a kind of civil war engineered by the British white rulers predominantly to weaken the power that the PPP Jagan party controlled. The British Prime Minister would engineer activities to determine the PPP maneuvers to govern, which led to civil unrest. British rulers ordered the arrest of Mr. and Mrs. Jagan and detained them in Brickdam Police Head Quarters. There were other civil uprisings taking place in the east coast sugar fields, with strikes and police intervention as well, along with civil unrest and military concerns on the sugar plantations.

During this tumultuous time, three Indian sugar workers were shot by Black police officers for being on the streets. Apparently the young boys were going to their homes after returning from the movie theater. The processions and emotional levels led to retaliation to the Black policemen who shot the Indians. Fighting became ubiquitous in Guyana. Some black men from Mackenzie mining town would harass and rape Indian women. News of this quickly reached the sugar cane

How I Became a Terrorist

workers in the India-populated plantation and villages and violence erupted everywhere.

Before long, civil unrest spread all over the country and racial tensions were at an all-time high. In Indian-populated villages with few black inhabitants, the Indians would burn the homes of Black families and mercilessly drive them out of the villages. Areas in which Indians were the minority saw the same problems. Blacks would beat Indians, burn their houses, rape their women and drive them out of the villages as well. This kind of civil uprising continued for some weeks until the British High Commissioner got British troops to come to Guyana and offered patrol in the country coastlines, giving some level of security and stability.

In 1964 I recall my first memory of feeling the effects of the chaos firsthand. I was with one of my elder sisters and brother playing in our neighbor's yard with his son and daughters. As we kicked a ball around the yard, we heard a bugle echoing through our village and we all stopped what we were doing and ran inside to safety. The bugle was our warning that Black uprising fighters were on the prowl in our village.

Although we were only playing two houses away on this particular day, we didn't have time to get to our home so we had to take refuge in our neighbor's house. After a while, things calmed down and we were able to leave the neighbor's and return to our home, but only when my father came to rescue us.

On that same evening we witnessed some homes of a black family burn to the ground. We knew the families, too. I went to school with the children who

Edan Ganie

lived in those houses and our parents worked together and were friends with their parents. Thus, that night my older brother, who was about seven, held my hand as we crawled to the very back of the yard under the coconut tree to watch the fire turn a very well-liked and respectable family's house into soot and ash. I was five when I tragically witnessed this horrifying event.

All the violence and terror within our community was done by the hands of a few. A handful of radicals from both the Black community and the Indian community were the instigators of hatred in the riots. Of course, the few fuming instigators were the ones queued by rage and motivated by their respective political leaders to promulgate the hate.

Shortly after this there was another fire on the same street. While I was clinging to my brother, we moved to the front of the yard, hiding between the beautiful flower trees my sister grew to get a closer look at the second flaming house. It was burnt to the ground by the time we saw it and people were scattered all over shouting and screaming. Some were stealing the burnt zinc sheets from the roof, taking them home where they would use them to repair and rebuild their own homes. The same thing was happening everywhere to Blacks and Indians alike depending on the location. It was common across the entire country while the "80 Days" Strike lasted. Eventually the strike was over and things calmed down a bit, but the peace was only momentary.

———

CHAPTER FIVE:

Bare Foot School Days

A few years after the 1964 "80 Days" Strike, things began to settle down and many who had left their homes, or traded homes with another, were finally returning. While the uprising was going on, Blacks who lived in Indian Villages would trade homes with an Indian friend in a Black village, and vice versa, for the sake of safety. After the uprising had finally come to an end and it was safe to do so, the respective Blacks and Indians returned to their rightly owned homes.

It was 1965 and things were starting to feel the way they did pre-uprising once again, somewhat. We were living in Plantation Tushcen, which was next to Plantation Vorgenoegen to the west. Vorgenoegen was where the primary school was. Vorgenoegen was a predominantly Black village, but my parents still decided to send my brothers and sisters to school there. Unfortunately the residue of the racial tension that swelled during the uprising still lingered a bit in the wake of the revolt and the effects trickled down to the children, which meant that there were some nasty fights between Black groups and Indian groups on a daily basis at school. It was normal for kids to have fights after school was closed in the afternoon. Day

Edan Ganie

after day, children would return home to their families with purpled eyes and swollen lips.

The sight of the scrapes and bruises on the children would spark residual anger left over from the uprising in their parents. At that point, adults would engage in village fights among themselves. Thus, the society became split to the point that one race did not trust the other.

To prevent some of these tensions, the elders of my village petitioned the government to open a primary school in Zeelugt, a primarily Indian-occupied community. Between the children of Zeelugt and the children of our village, there were arguably enough students to start a primary school. The elders won their case and the government provided some teachers, along with some volunteer teachers, to begin a school that would include around 300 students.

There were no buildings to the school and no classrooms; the classes were held beneath the houses of some of the volunteers' homes from the community in Zeelugt Village. The houses were built on stilts that were eight to ten feet tall, so students would gather beneath them for their lessons. The conditions were somewhat primitive, but at the very least children were getting the chance at an education without daily violence.

When rain fell, the water would accumulate under the benches and tables in the classrooms. The floors of the classrooms were filled with saw dust that volunteer parents would bring in to try to keep the area as dry as possible. Ornery boys found a way to take advantage of rainy days, though. When the rain would start to

How I Became a Terrorist

come into the classroom and accumulate, some of the boys would take out rulers and provide the water a flat surface to travel down so it would rise faster. When it reached a certain level, our feet would get wet.

"Miss," a boy would call out as his hand shot in the air. "My feet are getting drenched," he'd say, peering down at his soggy feet.

Our teacher would come and inspect the level of dampness and the amount of water pooling at our bare feet and if she thought it was enough, we'd all be dismissed for the day. Once she made the call, we were free to stomp in the puddles and splash around in the trenches. The village was our water park.

You see, up until the 1980's, most people in the lower cast in society could not even afford to wear shoes, so we were particularly subject to the weather around us. A lot of school children (including myself) had only one uniform to wear to school. At our school, Zeelugt Primary School, girls had to wear a pink blouse and a green skirt, and boys wore khaki pants and a cream shirt, but there were no codes for shoes because most of us couldn't afford them anyway. Whoever could afford them wore them, but most could not.

A lot of the students wore slippers in place of shoes, but my family didn't even have the means to provide me with those. I had calluses on my feet from running two miles every day to and from school. The road I ran on wasn't even paved, either. It was a brick road and had rocks scattered on it's surface that would often times get lodged in a heel or the ball of a foot. We would pick the rocks out and bleed while we ran, and often the

Edan Ganie

rocks would leave scars behind. Not many feet escaped my village without plenty of scars.

Our feet would also take a beating when the fruit trees were in bloom. My siblings and I, along with almost all the kids in the village, would scurry up and down fruit trees that stood in the abandoned sugar estate yards and collect the sweet, ripe fruit that hung from the branches. There were mangoes, guava, star apple, tangerines, coconuts; all begging for us to pluck them from their birthplace on those trees, and so we did without hesitation. We came out with more than mangoes, though. More times than not, a sharp branch would pierce a big toe or a splinter of wood from the bark of the tree would slide into the flesh of our feet. We would climb the trees and it would cause us cuts and calluses to our feet. It could be a painful exploit, climbing those trees, but one well worth the added scars.

So, without shoes on my feet, I got myself to and from school daily (and up fruit trees when there was a reward to be had). We had a small farm, and I would go to school while my older brothers helped out on the farm. It was a lot of work for everyone, but with my mom, dad, and older siblings all pitching in, I was able to go to school instead of spend my days in the field. I still had a lot of chores to do, but I was also able to go to get an education.

My mother was the one who took lead coordinating the work on the farm. As I said, my brothers worked out with the livestock and crops. My sisters, however, rarely went to the farm. They would go occasionally when we had large crops to reap or for an outing on a

How I Became a Terrorist

Sunday, but they were normally preoccupied at home with cleaning and cooking. My mom had done a great job working out the division of labor.

My father became ill in his fifties and could not work anymore. He was given pension, which was barely enough for his sustenance, let alone an entire family's. My older brothers were married by that time and had their own home and families, so they couldn't take over the family farm. They tried to help my parents and the remaining four of us that were still at home by coming out on weekends and in the evenings, but could only do so much.

The struggle to support our family became more and more difficult. The farm needed someone other than my mother to help do the physical things. In short, the farm needed a man, someone to take my dad's place to help my mother with what she was unable to handle. Labor was not always reliable for farm projects and my mother did not have the ability to manage the process on her own. My brother and I, we were thirteen and fifteen at the time and I was the younger, tried taking days off from school to help on the farm.

My brother and I tried to alternately skip school and work with my mother on the farm, but our answer did not solve the problem. We needed to be there full time if we were to have any chance at making a living. Hence, my brother, Omar, dropped out of school at sixteen and began working on the farm full time. This was our bread budget. We depended on the farm income. Even with Omar working fulltime, though, it was hard to make things work properly.

45

Edan Ganie

I always had a strong desire to not only go to school, but to finish my secondary education and go on to college. I wasn't the most disciplined student in the world and I probably played a bit more than I should have, but I always did well in school and it was something I loved. It came natural to me. In fact, after a year or so after Omar had to quit school, I finished writing my College of Preceptors (CP) exams and I did very well on them. I always did well on my exams.

You could say I was better than a mediocre student. I was within the top 5 percent of the class. There were always a group of students who would compete with me for the top grade in the class. Sometimes I would drop out of this race and fall back to about fifth, but I was never at the bottom.

Although school was my dream, I knew that my family needed my help. I tried to get a job after my writing exam but there were none available. I also needed to study for the general certificate exam (GCE), which is equivalent to a high school diploma and would prepare me for college. As much as I yearned to go on in my studies though, I couldn't afford to pay for classes to write the exam. Tuition at the Universal College was $25 per quarter and my parents couldn't afford it.

I ended up taking a scholarship entrance exam and I did outstanding, which meant I would be given one year free tuition. I was ecstatic about that, but I failed to see the big picture. This was a private school with children from wealthy families. The uniforms there wouldn't be like the ones in my neighboring village. They would have strict dress codes with ties and shoes,

How I Became a Terrorist

and we didn't have the money for any of it. Along with this, I'd have to buy my own books, and I certainly didn't have the money for school text books. With the cost of tuition, the cost of traveling, the cost of clothes, and the loss of my wages, it was just too much for my family.

When I went to primary school, I wore the same uniform every day. When it was dirty, my sisters washed it in the evening for me to wear the next day. To get a new uniform, I would have to wait until the next school year when my mother would customarily buy us new uniforms. The old uniform I had I wore at home to replace the one pair of torn pants I owned that showed my butt cheeks when I walked in the road. I never even wore underwear because we could not afford it, so private school seemed a little out of reach.

I did attend the Universal College in 1974 with a full scholarship for one year. I studied this year, wrote my CP exams, but could not continue school for financial reasons.

I remember one day after the school year ended, during summer vacation when I had just returned home from a day's work on the farm with my mother and brother. We sat on a long wooden beach we had downstairs enjoying the cool afternoon breeze and recapping the days work with my folks. I looked up the street and saw my principal walking towards our house. The last thing I wanted to do was face him. I was ashamed that I couldn't afford to return to school, so I excused myself and waited in my room upstairs.

I went to my room and waited to hear what my principal was there to talk about. I suspected it was about

47

Edan Ganie

me going back to school. Since my room was directly above where they sat, I could hear the conversation. I eavesdropped on them, which I know wasn't polite, but I did.

"It would be a mistake for you not to send Edan back to school," my principal explained. "He is doing so well and he has an excellent head for education." With that, he handed my mother a piece of paper. It was my certificate for the CP. I had passed.

"Do you know what this is?" he asked. My mother nodded as she pulled the paper to her chest. "He is a bright boy."

"I know he is," my mother said. "But we have to have him here to help us. He needs to help his brother on the farm."

"I understand it is hard,' my principal said, "but he could do something much more with his life if he would go to school."

"I would love for him to be able to, but we just can't afford it," my mother replied.

"Just promise me you'll at least consider what I've said," the principal finally said to my mother.

"I will consider it," my mom agreed, but I knew that there was nothing to be considered.

I was fourteen at the time and I never went back to school, not in Guyana anyway. I couldn't even afford to buy a text book. All I could afford the year I went was one notebook. I immediately became a fulltime farmer assisting my folks with all the chores that needed to be done. I worked the fields with my older brother and assisted my mom in getting vegetables to the market.

How I Became a Terrorist

I also went to the Zeeburg market with my mother to sell produce every Saturday.

Our farm was about five miles away from home. There were three main modes of transportation to the farm, walking, a donkey cart, and my dad's bicycle. My brother and I would use my father's bicycle when only the two of us went on the trip and we would have the donkey cart to transport the produce to the market. We would take turns towing each other on the bicycle bars. Sometimes when the wind was high along the seaside road we would both pedal together. My brother would sit on the seat and I would put my feet on both sides over the bar. And this is how my life was for some time, going to and from the farm every day—nothing but farming.

A few months after the principal had visited I took a job with a timber company as a welder and went to work in Guyana's rain forest. I enjoyed the job and worked there for six months. I saved all my money and brought it home for my parents to plough the farm and plant more crops. I stayed a month and helped my brother finish planting the crops and then returned to work.

While I was at home for that month I wrote for the police exam. I was called in for an interview with the criminal investigation division in Leonora Station. I was interviewed by a detective sergeant, and I thought the interview went rather well, but then things went south.

"You said you're a farmer?" the detective said to me. "What kind?"

49

Edan Ganie

"We have a small provision farm," I explained. "We have pumpkins, corn, rice, cows; just provisions."

"You think you could get me a half bag of rice and some provisions?" he asked with one eyebrow reaching for his hairline.

"That would be difficult for me," I explained, fidgeting in my chair. "My family is having a hard time growing rice to feed ourselves. I'm very sorry."

I never heard from him again.

So, I spent the better part of the seventies working to help support my family and then something big happened. My brother, Osman, migrated to America and joined the United States Army.

CHAPTER SIX:

Coming to America

In the seventies things took a turn for the worse for Guyana with Prime Minister Forbes Burnham becoming more autocratic by the day and also bringing heat on Guyana by making deals with certain countries. With Burnham's iron hand on the country, a mass exodus occurred because nobody wanted to stick around to see how much worse it could get with Burnham and his thugs ruling the country with absolute power, absolute corrupt power at that.

Osman was a prayer answered for all of us. He had migrated to the United States and joined the army and at about the time I had tried (and failed) to become a policeman, he had already been in the U.S. Army for three years and was made a sergeant. He was a crew chief with the rotary wing division in Fort Lewis, Washington.

Osman was able to sponsor our entire family so that we could get Visas to migrate to the US. One year after he started his sponsorship, we received a very formal looking, government issued notification in the mail that said that we were to respond to the US embassy in Guyana after we had filled out and submitted all

Edan Ganie

the forms enclosed. We did just as the letter said, and then waited.

Getting a Visa is no quick process, so it was another year before we heard anything again from the Embassy. Finally when we'd already made our way through all four seasons again, we received notification to get our medical records prepared and our medical exams completed. Again, we did just as we were instructed, and two months later we were called for an interview. We were asked things about where we were going and what we planned to do. Where would we live? Would we be seeking employment? Osman was the answer to most of the questions, and that must've been the right answer because we were finally given our visas to travel.

I had two weeks to get everything ready. I went in to the British Overseas Airways Corporation (BOAC) office in Georgetown, the capital of Guyana, with my mom and bought my ticket. It was 1978, and at nineteen years old, I was going to leave Guyana for good to become a US citizen and maybe get that better life that my grandparents had chased to Guyana.

"Where will you be travelling. Mr. Ganie?" the ticket clerk asked.

"I'd like to go to Washington," I told her with a nervous smile. I'd never flown anywhere before.

"Okay. You're flight to Washington D.C. will be leaving on Tuesday, September 15, at 9 a.m.," she said as she clicked away at her keyboard. The fact that she said Washington *D.C.* didn't even register to me. I had no idea there was a difference between Washington and Washington D.C.

52

How I Became a Terrorist

"Thank you so much," I said, taking my ticket and ID from the woman. We exchanged smiles and my mother and I left the place, none the wiser.

Two weeks later I was back at the Timehri Airport to go to what I thought was Washington State, but was actually Washington D.C. I would be flying to New York via the BOAC, so even as I waved goodbye to my family, I hadn't a clue I had bought a ticket to the wrong Washington.

I landed in JFK, still unaware of my error. After clearing immigrations and customs, I went to the BOAC counter to pick up my boarding pass to Washington. I had a little time to spare between flights, so I thought I'd call Osman to let him know that I was on American soil.

"I am finally here," I said after Osman said hello into the phone.

"That is great news, brother. Great news," Osman replied.

"I'm at JFK Airport now," I told him. "I will be landing in Washington in about an hour it looks like."

"Wait, how will you be here in one hour?" Osman said back quickly.

"Because I am at JFK and it says the flight is no more than an hour."

"Oh no," Osman sighed. "You are flying to Washington D.C., but I live in Washington State."

"There are two Washingtons?" I asked.

"There are," he said. "I didn't even think to say anything about it. Why would they fly you to D.C. if you said Washington anyway?"

53

Edan Ganie

"I don't know," I said shaking my head. "I said Washington to the clerk, and that is all I said."

"Just go to the counter and see if they can switch it," Osman suggested.

We hung up and I went over to the counter, a little disoriented by everything going on.

"Excuse me," I said to a woman looking down at her computer screen. "I bought a ticket in Guyana, where I am from, but they made my ticket to Washington D.C. and I need to go to Washington State where my brother is waiting for me."

"Do you have your boarding pass?" the woman asked without any facial expression what-so-ever.

"Here it is," I said as I handed it to her.

"It looks like that is how you purchased your ticket, Mr. Ganie, so there is nothing that we can do. I'm sorry," she said as she handed me my ticket back and continued staring at her screen.

I walked away from the woman more confused than ever. I didn't understand why they couldn't just switch me to another flight, but it was obvious that wasn't going to happen, so I called Osman again.

"Any luck?" he asked.

"None," I said. "They say they can't do anything for me.

"I was afraid of that," he said.

"What can I do now?"

"Go find a hotel for the night." Osman said. "We have plenty of family there. I'll get someone to pick you up in the morning to take you back to the airport. You can get a flight to Washington *STATE* then. Not here

How I Became a Terrorist

an hour and you're causing problems, little brother," Osman laughed a little.

I took a cab to a nearby hotel and spent the night doing something I had never done before. I watched a television and enjoyed air conditioning. I flipped through the channels and was baffled at how many choices there were. I wasn't familiar with any television shows, so everything was brand new to me. I also took a nice hot shower and then I went to bed.

In the morning I got up and had a little breakfast in the dining area as I waited for a family member to come save me. I saw my cousin walk into the lobby and I rushed out to meet him. It was nice to see a familiar face in such an unfamiliar place.

"A good lesson in US geography I guess," my cousin joked. Everyone seemed to think this was funny but me.

My cousin drove me back to the airport and went with me to buy my ticket. This time I went Northwest Orient. We purchased a ticket to Seattle, Washington, and in two hours I was on my way to my new homeland. I have been living in Washington State ever since that day, thirty-five years ago.

When I arrived in Washington, Osman and his two-year-old daughter were there waiting. We hugged and I gave my niece a kiss. It was the first time I'd ever seen her in person. With our greetings out of the way, we went to the baggage claim to get my one bag.

"You travel heavy," my brother joked.

"I don't have much to pack," I replied with a smile.

I loaded my bag in his car and we were off, off to a new life. We drove to Fort Lewis, where my brother

Edan Ganie

and his family lived on the military post. He was an infantry man and would often spend weeks in the fields for training, so I was on my own a lot of the time from the very beginning. I was new in a country where I was quickly learning the culture. It was different than back home, but I was catching on.

The moment I stepped foot on Washington soil I was off to find a job. I didn't know what I would be qualified for with my limited education, but I wasn't going to stop searching until someone had said, "you're hired." I was relentless, and relentlessly disappointed, for the first weeks. I went from place to place filling out applications and sitting through interviews with management. I often would walk about the post and look for work. After seven weeks of job hunting, I began to get a little frustrated with the process. If this was the land of opportunity, I wanted to know where I needed to go to find it.

Finally, after searching and filling out a pile of applications for jobs that would never be mine, I was offered a job at the Army Commissary bagging groceries and carrying them out to people's cars for them. It wasn't glamorous by any stretch of the imagination, but I made twenty or thirty dollars a day and that was enough to keep a roof over my family's head and food in the cabinets.

There were about forty checkout counters to serve the military and their families who shop on post. We were paired in teams of two for each checkout register. One of us would bag the groceries the cashier stacked on the counter and when the groceries were bagged,

How I Became a Terrorist

one of us would push the shopping carts to the parking lot for the customer and put all their bags away in their vehicles for them. We were paid with tips.

In my first day of work at the Commissary, I was teamed up with a kid named Jim. We were about the same age. I was just a year older than Jim, who just finished high school. He was going to community college in the mornings and worked in the afternoons. Jim and I hit it off immediately and over the years became great friends. Jim became my first friend in America. He was the person who taught me most about American culture, introducing me to the movies, taking me to ball games, and even inviting me to family events. Jim and I have remained close friends to this day. That grocery bagging job was a real lucky thing for me as it turned out.

It felt good, like I was finally finding a place for myself in my new home. I had a job, my family, and now a friend.

So, I spent some time bagging cereal and bread, milk and eggs, living on the tips that people gave me for carrying their groceries to their car, but eventually I wanted to move on to something better than that. I didn't want to have to rely on tips only forever, so I set out to find another job and I did, at a nursing home washing dishes. Again, it wasn't going to keep me in furs, but it paid a little more than my grocery bagging job and it was more consistent, so I thought it was a step in the right direction. By this time I knew my little brother and sister would be coming over soon, so

Edan Ganie

I knew that I was going to have to move into jobs that would pay more to help with their transition.

While I was working as a dishwasher, our family faced another serious blow. My mom was diagnosed with cancer. That meant that both my parents were sick now, so it was more important than ever that I did whatever I could to help them. Neither could work and they both needed medical attention, so I was going to have to do even more to bring in extra income. I decided that I'd get a second job.

With both my parents sick and my siblings coming arrival on the brain, I scoured the classified looking for another job to take on. Finally I saw it, "PLUMBER ASSISTANT WANTED: NO EXPERIENCE NEEDED."

Perfect, I thought, and I called the number on the AD and made an appointment to meet with the plumber immediately. We met in his makeshift office that was cluttered floor to ceiling with papers. He was an older man with a kind face and eyebrows that must have been getting more unruly with his birthdays. The plumber's name was Eugene, but he went by only "Gene," he told me.

"I'm gonna tell you son, this isn't going to be fun work to do," Gene warned.

"That's no problem for me, sir," I assured him. "I once worked on a plantation, so I'm not afraid of dirty jobs."

"What I do is install plumbing into mobile homes and what I'll need you to do is crawl underneath all the homes to place the pipes. I'm getting too old for all

How I Became a Terrorist

that," he chuckled. "That sound like something you'd be interested in?"

"Yes sir," I said.

"Well, if you're ready you can start tomorrow."

And with that, I had my second job that had me crawling around in the dirt under mobile homes all day.

————

CHAPTER SEVEN:

Making Cheese

With two jobs, I was making more money, but I couldn't help but think I was capable of doing more than rolling around in the dirt and scraping leftover meatloaf off of cafeteria trays. I also couldn't help but think that I'd never get to college if I was working two jobs the rest of my life, and college was a part of my American dream. Luckily for me, there happened to be a woman I met in the nursing home who thought I was capable of more than scrubbing dishes, too. Her name was Mary and she worked with me in the nursing home.

"Why are you a dishwasher, Edan?" Mary asked me one day as she was walking through the kitchen.

"I don't know what you mean," I answered.

"I mean you're such a hard worker. Why don't you do something else?"

"I would if I could," I told her. "If you have something in mind let me know and I'll gladly do it."

"I do actually," Mary said. "My husband works out at the cheese factory. What do you think about me talking to him?"

"I'd be beyond thankful," I told her.

"That's what we'll do then," Mary said.

Edan Ganie

Mary was true to her word. She talked to her husband and he got me the job making eight dollars and hour at the factory. I worked nonstop once I was hired. If a shift needed covered, I was the man to do it. When everyone else wanted off for holidays, I was there working away. Eight dollars was a lot for me back in 1979 and I would work as many hours as they'd let me.

I worked as hard as I could at the cheese factory. Making cheese was a skillful job as well as a physically demanding one. The factory was antique and the art of making cheese was done the old fashioned way. There was nothing high-tech or automated about it. It required a lot of back breaking physical work but I was young, physically fit and motivated to work hard.

At first, I was placed on the "grave yard" shift, where all new workers start on a temporary basis because of the union and seniority. The graveyard crew was a rogue group of guys who were there because they avoided management and got away with things they couldn't dream of on the day shift.

As the new kid on the block, I was given all the grunt work. I was assigned the "brine" jobs. This is the area where mozzarella cheeses were placed in cargo stainless steel tanks that were full of brine, or chilled water below 40 degrees that have a very high salt content. After the mozzarella cheese is processed out of a machine it is placed in cooling tank of water to harden. After about twenty minutes in the holding tank, it is taken and placed in the brine tanks to absorb the salt that is placed on top of the cheese. Every hour or so I was required to turn the cheese in the cold water

How I Became a Terrorist

and salt it again. It was grueling. I wore an apron and a pair of thick gloves to keep my hands warm and I would stand about six of my eight hours per shift processing mozzarella cheese in those soggy, freezing conditions.

I was willing to do all the work the other guys on the shift avoided and I never complained. I would often work overtime to help day shift catch up when the operation was running behind. The plant manager took notice of this and would put me to work on the day shift when necessary. I quickly became the fill-in person for the day shift when workers would go on vacations or when anyone was sick. This meant that sometimes I was working back to back shifts or only getting a few hours between my graveyard shift and my day shift.

When the other guys would complain and demand overtime, I kept quiet. I was just happy to have a job and to be making enough money to help my family. My relentless work ethic and my gratitude for the work paid off fast. Within a month, I was asked if I wanted to learn to make cheese. This was the highest paid job in the factory.

Within a year I was promoted and was assisting the production manager. I got a decent raise and I was finally at a point where I could help my family and go to college, so at twenty-four years old I went to the community college and enrolled in my first semester of school.

I began taking classes for a degree in Business Management. I started to work during the day and went to school at night, and that is how I began to

63

Edan Ganie

really succeed in my new life as an American. I would volunteer to work all extra hours or shifts that I could and fill in for anyone who wanted a day off. I would even work for foremen during holidays. I would work and punch their timecards and they would pay me when they received their checks. I didn't let school slow me down at work.

After six years of work at the cheese factory, I earned my degree in business. Coincidently, the factory was sold around the same time and the owner wanted to break the union. There were various cat and mouse games taking place between management and the union during this time. The final play was the union called a strike and management replaced all the workers who were on the line.

Fortunately, or unfortunately, at the time of the strike, I was on workers compensation as a result of an injury to my back. I had herniated two discs while working. I did not have to join the strike but would spend time on the picket line supporting its cause.

CHAPTER EIGHT:

Becoming an Entrepreneur

Within a few months of the strike I was recovering from my injury nicely and continued with my schooling. Just a year after the strike ended, I earned my BA degree and enrolled in the MBA program. I also began working for the State of Washington as an Accountant.

I worked for the state of Washington in three agencies in various positions. My career took a turn for the better in 1988 when I was given the opportunity to work with a team that was undertaking healthcare reform for the state. My task on the small team of five was to take lead for writing the "waivers" that would permit the state of Washington to deviate from the prescribed manner the federal government allowed states to spend federal money to purchase health care for Medicaid patients.

This job fell right in line with my career path. Prior to taking the position, I worked with the state hospital administration with reimbursement payments. I also worked in prior positions that were related to nursing home administration payment reimbursement and analysis. Along with my work in the medical field and reimbursements, I held positions that dealt with

Edan Ganie

financial analysis and payments for physicians and other healthcare providers for government programs. The new job couldn't have been more perfect for me, or I for it. Working with the healthcare reform team provided me the opportunity to use my healthcare work experience, while also implementing my degrees in Business and Finance. In addition to that, I was completing my second MBA in Healthcare Administration at the time.

I was given the lead in drafting the core set of healthcare services that would be covered under the Washington State waiver program approved by the federal government. I participated in endless community meetings with hospital administration employees, physicians, and other healthcare providers in Washington, as well as insurance company representatives and other community advocates, as we crafted the program that would then take half a million federal and state funded healthcare patients that were enrolled in what was then the 1990's cutting edge, "managed care" health care program. The shift from traditional fee-for-service payment to the new managed care program realized significant savings. At the same time it increased access to care for patients who were originally without a primary care physician and paired them with physicians who now were managing all aspects of their healthcare. I felt I was following in my father's footsteps in some ways.

While I was developing the program for the government, I met with stakeholders from all parts of the community, including HMOs, hospitals, physicians, nursing homes, surgery centers, etc. I was honored

How I Became a Terrorist

to have several job offers from the various sects of healthcare, and I accepted one from an organization that wanted to start a HMO. I saw in the job a unique opportunity to experience all phases of a start up company.

I served in several positions with the Ethix Northwest, which was an administration service organization that was going through the application process for an HMO license. I was Director of Operations, which was a position that proved to have its own unique set of challenges. We were integrating everything in the company: finance, organizational structure, contracting, personnel and human resources—everything. I had a hand in absolutely every part of the restructuring, and no detail was too small for me.

For a couple of years, we were the largest contractor to Washington State for its government programs contract. The company experienced significant growth, all the while experiencing some momentous pitfalls. I went on to serve as the Executive Director, which presented me with some challenging moments in our growth cycle. I worked with the CEO to build a new information system that provided unique financial reports needed to manage the risks the company was undertaking. It was a success and it saved our company. We became a reputable player in the new environment of managed care.

We attracted a lot of attention and New York Life healthcare ended up swooping us up. We were quickly merged with several other similar sister companies and became a national healthcare company. In a couple of

Edan Ganie

years we sold the company to Aetna Healthcare. All of the wheeling and dealing provided me with priceless exposure to the start up, growth, and success of a company. It inspired me to become an entrepreneur, something that was always in me since I was a child growing up on the farm.

In 1997 with $25,000, I launched A Healthcare Company, an administrative services organization predominantly for workers compensation injury claims. With the support and expertise of my two brothers, who had a combined forty years of industry experience, we quickly became one of the top three contractors in the state of Washington for workers compensation programs for independent examination for injury claims.

As the president and CEO, I was in the field quite regularly as a hands-on-manager. We served the pacific Northwest region and had operations in Washington, Alaska, Oregon, Idaho and Montana regions. Thus began my frequent flying, which led to the Alaska Airlines incident in 2003.

Within a decade I grew the company into a multimillion dollar company. We engaged the services of over sixty physicians, over twenty private contractors, and twelve administrative support staffs. With the success of this company I began diversifying into other industries and looking into international businesses. Over the years I invested in healthcare, technology, mining, agriculture, and real estate (commercial and residential).

How I Became a Terrorist

With my business ventures reaching out across the oceans, over the years, I have become acutely conscious of the changing world, particularly the economy in the various countries that I have traveled over the past decade. These include Asia, Africa, Europe, Middle East, North America and South America. I have traveled to many international destinations for business and personal vacations with my family. I frequent Asia for business and over the years I have developed an affinity for the Asian culture. The people are friendly and very courteous. I also like the topography of the Asian continent and find myself visiting the countryside when I am there. I also always like to pay keen attention to the various industries and how they have emerged in the developing countries for my own business ventures.

As I have grown as an entrepreneur, I have become increasingly aware of the economic and social transformations that have been taking place around the world. With a mind for constant expansion, I began looking for business opportunities in the places I like to visit, and eventually I developed businesses in Asia, Africa, and South America. I then integrated these operations with the existing business I have in the United States.

As my businesses evolved, I began travelling more frequently to the countries in which I conduct business and also visiting other countries every chance I get and this is where my story returns to the beginning chapters. You see, that run-in with the officers at SeaTac in 2003 wasn't the last time that I felt the iron hand of discrimination pound down on me while traveling. In

69

Edan Ganie

fact, that experience was only a glimpse of what was to come for me, but my hope is this book will help bring my awful experiences to an end, not just for me, but for every Muslim everywhere who faces the same pointless discrimination, the same bigotry, that has been solidly in place since the day that a few vile, wicked people executed those despicable acts that shook our nation to the core. Muslims everywhere have been paying for those acts, and it is time that the prejudice and Islamaphobia is exposed and that we as a people do something about it.

CHAPTER NINE:

We have to Comply, Period

Since the time I was just a child, I have loved to travel. Whether by plane, train, or donkey, traveling has always intrigued me. In my small plantation village that consisted of only 100 families, there was only one tiny grocery store that carried only the necessities and two rum shops. We didn't even have a school in my village, which made traveling a necessity. Traveling far, however, wasn't always an option.

In such a small community with so little luxury, entertainment was sparse. The only recreation, if you could consider it as such, was a plot of land that the plantation owner had provided to the villagers to serve as a cricket field. There were no movie theaters, arcades, skating rinks, or even a basketball or tennis court anywhere near; just a plot of open space for us to play cricket.

Tuschen was only about twenty miles away from the city, but twenty miles may as well be a thousand when you have no motor vehicles, and no one in our village, save the plantation owners, had them. Because we did not have access to cars or motorbikes, the only mode of transportation from my village to the city was a train

Edan Ganie

and a few taxi cars. The train cost money, too, so it was only on special occasions that we would get to take it. It was such a rarity for my family to have enough extra money to take the train that I didn't see the city until I was nine years old.

When I heard that we would be taking a trip on the train, my heart raced in my chest. I had only been to neighboring villages for school or to sell our produce. I had only dreamt of what the city was like. It wasn't just the city itself that I was fascinated with though; it was the landscape along the way.

Even as a young boy, I was intrigued with the vast landmarks along the countryside. From the very first time I rode that wheezing, barreling train twenty miles into the main city, I fell in love with the beauty of the land. Staring out the window became as enjoyable to me as the trip itself. I never lost that love for diverse landscapes and mesmerizing topography. Before I ever stepped foot on an airplane, I would fantasize about seeing everything from a bird's eye view: the mountains, the streams and rivers, the rolling of the land.

As I rode the bus, taxi, or train, I took in all the sites around me. I never wanted to waste a moment dozing or chatting; I wanted to take in the scenery and notice the subtle changes of the land as I went. To this day I am observant of my surroundings and learn from my travels. I consider it a real treat every time I visit anywhere. I consider my travels, whether for pleasure or business, a form of recreation. Because I have always had such a passion for traveling and new scenery, I have counted myself extremely fortunate that

How I Became a Terrorist

my work affords me the opportunity to travel the globe. I treasure each and every chance I get to visit a different country, or even a different part of the United States.

The traveling part of my business has always given me a real sense of gratification, as I have been able to further my success while seeing the world. I have always considered my business travels a reward to myself for having worked so hard to develop my many companies. It is something I find mighty enjoyable and best of all, my travels are "gratis persona," and also a perk of my labor. Unfortunately some noticeable differences have occurred during my travels over the past decade, especially in the United States, and those differences have been drastically altering my experiences.

Since 9-11 and my first run-in with airport security at SeaTac, travelling has become as much a source of anxiety, agitation, and humiliation as it has been a source of pleasure for me. Where I once felt only excitement at the prospect of flying, particularly overseas to places like China and Thailand, I now feel a twinge of apprehension as I enter airports. I can no longer sit back and relax while I trot the globe, and I am not the only one experiencing these kinds of changes.

In response to the terrorist attacks waged by religious extremists on that fateful day in September more than a decade ago, the authorities in the United States have adopted, implemented and enforced strict security measures to fight terrorism in its efforts to protect its citizens and the national border. I am in utter agreement that we must take precautionary steps to protect ourselves from any horrific repetition of 9-11, or

Edan Ganie

any other slighter attempts by terrorists meant to cause harm to innocent people. I, like almost every other American, see the need for stricter security measures at airport borders and public places. I understand that longer waits, lengthy lines, the near strip searches that each traveler is subject to before entering the terminal are only there to protect the innocent.

Although these things are time-consuming and can be a little frustrating, I am more than willing to do each of them if it means that we will all be safer. I am even more than cooperative when I am pulled aside by security personnel and law enforcement officers to undergo a more thorough search and further questioning. However, I began to notice a very distinct and discriminating pattern of profiling as I travelled.

My earliest encounters of security profiling began shortly after the twin towers were toppled by terrorists in September of 2001. In Chapter Two, I provided an account in September 2003 in which my nephew, brother, and I were escorted off a plane not once, but twice for reasons that were never clear. That wasn't the very first time that I had been subject to that kind of profiling, however.

I often travel to Asia for business. On July 1, 2003, a business acquaintance, Mr. Aly, who is of Asian decent, and I were returning home from a trip to Bangkok, Thailand. At this point, I was accustomed to travelling without incident, so I entered the airport without expectation of a problem, but a problem I soon would find.

How I Became a Terrorist

Although Mr. Aly was a resident of the United States, he also kept a home in Bangkok, where we would often stay during our business trips to the area. Not only did it make travelling less expensive, it was also conveniently located near the airport. On this July morning we had a check-in of 4 a.m., so Mr. Aly's home was a real blessing to us.

On the morning of July 1, we left his home before the sun had made its way to our part of the globe and we headed to Suvarnabhumi Airport, which is Bangkok's international airport. Once we had arrived and checked our bags, we went to the airport's prayer hall to do our morning prayers. Bangkok airports, like many airport hubs around world with high traffic of Muslim travelers, offer a "Musullah," an exclusive area in the airport where Muslim men and women are appropriately accommodated for their prayers. So, we did our prayers and then headed for the Northwest Airline ticket counter to pick up our boarding passes.

It was early, so the airport was a little less crowded than usual. There were still plenty of travelers heading out on early flights, just like Mr. Aly and I, but there was a little less chaos and the lines weren't as long as they tended to be for afternoon flights, so the atmosphere seemed a bit more peaceful, until it was our turn at the ticket counter.

"Good morning," the flight attendant working the ticket counter said to Mr. Aly and me. "Where are we travelling today?"

"Seattle, Washington," I said as I reached in my coat pocket for my passport.

Edan Ganie

"And do we have our passports ready?" the woman asked, her bright pink lips smiling at the two of us.

"Here you are," I said as I placed my passport on the counter. Mr. Aly had his passport as well and lay in next to mine so we could both get our boarding passes.

The woman tapped away at her keyboard and as she did I could see her forehead wrinkle beneath her yellow-brown hair. She looked up at me and down at the screen once, and her brow furrowed yet again. It didn't usually take so long to get a boarding pass, so that coupled with the woman's expression told me that something was going on.

"Mr. Ganie, I need you to step aside please," the flight attendant finally said.

"Okay," I said.

"Would you like me to as well?" Aly asked the flight attendant.

"No, sir," she told him. "I just need Mr. Ganie. Here is your boarding pass."

"I'll just wait with you," Aly said to me as he waited for his boarding pass. "Surely this won't take long."

The flight attendant gave Aly his boarding pass and then called for airport security. I had no idea what was happening, but I stayed quiet while I waited for some kind of an explanation. The flight attendant never turned to tell me anything, though. She simply continued checking other passengers in, checking passports, and doling out boarding passes. One after another, I saw men and women passing through, but not a single person besides me was asked to step aside. I was starting to feel a little nervous about why I had

How I Became a Terrorist

been singled out and when someone was going to tell me what this was about.

"Do you know what this is about?" Aly asked fifteen minutes into our wait.

"I have no idea," I told him as I glanced down at my watch. "I hope it doesn't take too much longer, though."

"Me too," Aly said as he scanned the airport.

We stood for half an hour with no idea why I was pulled from the line or whom I was waiting for. My worry nearly lapsed into panic, as I knew that my flight would be leaving within the hour. If no one had even addressed me in the thirty minutes I'd been standing there, I couldn't imagine how long whatever came next would take.

Just as I was about to ask the flight attendant if she could tell me what was going on, I saw a security officer approaching, a young woman. The security officer and the flight attendant exchanged a few quick words and then the security officer came over to where I was standing.

"My name is Officer Montri and I'm with airport security," the woman said as she approached. "I need your passport please, Mr. Ganie." "Absolutely," I replied. "Can you tell me what is going on?"

"I'll be right back," she said as she took my passport, avoiding my question altogether.

So, she was off without supplying any details as to why she needed my ID, and Aly and I were left standing there in total confusion yet again. About ten minutes later she returned.

77

Edan Ganie

"I am going to need your driver's license. Mr. Ganie," she said to me this time.

I took my wallet out of my coat pocket again and fished out my driver's license. I didn't say anything to the officer this time or even attempt to get any more information since my last effort was useless. When she walked away, Aly and I turned to each other.

"Why does she want your driver's license?" Aly asked.

"I have no idea," I replied. "I've never had someone ask for it before."

"Neither have I," Aly said. "What could they even need it for? You aren't driving anywhere. We're flying home."

"This is strange," I said after I stood and thought for a moment.

"Indeed it is," Aly agreed. "And why don't they tell us anything? You would think they would explain some things while they are asking you for all this."

"You would think so," I said as I stared off in the distance. "I have a U.S. passport and I am going back home to the States on an American flight. This just doesn't make any sense at all."

"I've flown this exact flight a thousand times and never seen anything like this," Aly added. We both shook our heads as we waited for the woman to return with my license and passport.

It was another fifteen minutes before the security officer returned a second time. This time, however, she was not alone. She was accompanied by a middle-aged gentleman that was a little taller than me and athletic built.

How I Became a Terrorist

"My name is Officer Rattanakosin," he introduced himself. "I'm Officer Montri's supervisor."

He looked down at my driver's license and then looked up at me. I assumed he was checking to see which of us was Edan Ganie.

"I have a few questions for you, Mr. Ganie," he said.

"Yes, sir," I complied.

"Where do you live?" he asked as he stared down at my license.

"Washington State," I told him.

"Can you confirm your address please, sir?" he asked. I felt like I was being interrogated for a crime all of a sudden. I gave him my home address.

"What are your reasons for travelling with us today?"

"I'm returning home from a business trip with my partner, Mr. Aly," I told him as I nodded over to Aly.

By this time all other passengers had checked in for the flight and the check-in area was clear save Aly, me, and the security officers. Our flight was scheduled to leave at 6:00 a.m., and it was half past five by that point, so Aly and I started to worry that we would miss our flight back home.

"You go ahead to the boarding gate," I told Aly. "There's no reason for us both to miss the flight.

"Nonsense," he said as he waved the idea away with a swipe of his hand. "I'll go when you are finished here. I'm not getting on the plane without you."

I had known Aly and his family for almost thirty years. He was about sixty years old at the time. We both settled in Washington when we emigrated from our homelands. He had always been a respectable

Edan Ganie

gentleman as long as I had known him, and he proved what a loyal friend he was that day when he refused to leave my side.

Because Aly had a place in Bangkok for so long, he spoke Thai fluently. I was getting nowhere with anyone, so Aly decided he would ask the officers in their native tongue what was going on.

"What is the matter here that Mr. Ganie needs so much questioning?" he asked the officer in Thai.

Unfortunately, Aly's attempts were as useless as my own. We were given no answers, but we were finally told to proceed to the boarding gate after I had been thoroughly questioned.

We went through immigration, cleared security and proceeded to the gate. But just before we got to the departure gate, we were stopped by security officers for a second time. Interestingly, it was Officer Montri and Officer Rattanakosin once again.

"I need you to step aside please, sir," Officer Rattanakosin said as he motioned me away from the line. I didn't say anything; I simply did as I was asked, but I hoped that this wouldn't take as long as it had before because if it did, we would not make the flight.

Luckily this encounter was much briefer than the last. I wasn't asked for my identification again or questioned this time. They took my bags, thoroughly searched everything, and then told me to proceed to board the plane.

I thought once I finally made it onboard the flight that the arbitrary integrations were over, but that wasn't the case. As soon as we exited the plane in Seattle, Aly

How I Became a Terrorist

and I were met and questioned by CBP officers once we cleared immigration.

"What were your reasons for travelling to Asia?" an officer asked with his hands on his hips.

"I was there for business," I explained again. "Aly here is my partner."

The questions went on, but not once was I offered an explanation as to why I had been stopped so many times in just one trip.

"What countries did you visit while you were there?"

"What kind of business do you own?"

"What kind of activities did you do while you visited?"

"Who did you meet while you were there?"

I had been travelling to the Asia for business for over a decade, and I jumped from one Asian country to another while there, but never have I encountered any difficulties by Immigration or Customs in any of the Asian countries. The only difficulties I have ever had with authorities arise upon my return to the United States.

Since July of 2003, I have experienced the same routine at the Bangkok Airport at least a half dozen times on my return home. Every time it is the same flight with Northwest Airlines (now Delta) and even the same security officer asking for my driver's license. Each and every time she takes my passport and license and then comes back after talking to her supervisor to clear me for the flight. Both she and her supervisor know me well now, but still they stop me and ask for my ID without fail.

Edan Ganie

It has happened so often that Aly and I even joke with the two security guards about our little routine. They both know that I am no threat and they know all the answers before I even give them. Once after we got to know one another, I asked, "Why is it that you all do this every time?"

"We're required by US authorities to do it," they explained as they shrugged their shoulders. "We have to comply, period."

———

CHAPTER TEN:

Profiling, TSA, and Secondary Screening

According to authorities responsible for airport security, secondary screenings employed at airport security checkpoints are based on random selection, which means they select passengers standing in line waiting to go through security to get to the terminal without any criteria or characteristics in place—the process is suppose to be indiscriminate. Once selected for a secondary screening, the supposedly randomly selected individual will have their bags and other personnel items thoroughly searched in addition to the standard screenings everyone is required to take.

The thoroughness and details of these additional screenings vary from airport to airport; they may consist of a personal pat down by security personnel, being sent through the full screening machine, and/or security personnel taking swipes of the passenger's items for "gun shot residue" (GSR). Along with being subject to additional screenings, the passenger chosen is subject to the gawks and stares of hundreds of other passengers looking on during the process.

Edan Ganie

Although the process can be timely and a bit uncomfortable for the individuals chosen, I have always valued what the TSA does to ensure the safety of the crews, passengers, and citizens as a whole. These precautionary methods offer me a stronger sense of security when I travel.

While I understand and appreciate the efforts that airport authorities are making to avoid threats, over the years I have come to realize that the selections may be less "random" than the powers that be would like us to believe, as I am somehow always selected for "random screenings" regardless of where I am or my destination. I have been pulled aside so consistently over the last decade that I have come to expect being selected for the secondary screenings. I have reached a point that, when flying, I psychologically prepare myself for the moment in which I am picked out of the line from the rest and thoroughly searched.

As much as we would all like to believe that secondary screenings are random, I believe anyone who travels often would agree that there are a certain criteria for those most often chosen to undergo the additional searches. Those standing in line that look to be of Middle Eastern decent, Indian or Pakistani, and are from a region which is profoundly Muslim, are more prone to these "random selections." For a man of Indian descent like myself, a secondary search is expected.

For people, men especially, who fit a certain description, being pulled aside by a TSA employee has become almost as routine as checking bags and walking

How I Became a Terrorist

through a metal detector. I know for myself, I have begun to take the time for the additional searches into account when I plan each of my trips because of this fact. And without fail, I am plucked from the line by airport security to have my bags rummaged through and a police-style pat down. Both by business associates and my family members have observed this when travelling with me. It has actually become so much a part of travelling for me that my daughter and wife are fearful that if they continue to take trips with me that they will be subject to the same treatment before long. Like me, they have come to believe that there is nothing random about the selection process, and they do not want to risk being put on the same list that I have somehow landed on.

Just to be sure that my hypothesis regarding the authority's deliberate choice in pulling me out from the rest of my fellow passengers was accurate, one day when travelling from the Seattle airport I decided to test the random secondary screening process. I was travelling with my two brothers, who are also of Indian descent and Muslim, like myself, and we decided that we would go through the lines separately instead of together, thus drawing less attention to ourselves. We wanted to test to see whether or not that three supposedly unrelated men would all be stopped because of the way they looked.

So, my brothers and I staggered ourselves throughout the line, letting 10 to 15 people divide each of us. Just as we suspected, each of us were picked out as we passed through security to go through additional searches.

Edan Ganie

There was nothing that suggested to the security personnel that the three of us were related in any way. We were chosen then, you would have to assume, because we looked to be of Middle eastern descent.

My brothers and I complied with the screening. After we had all had our bags opened and rifled through and had roaming hands check us for anything we might be hiding, we met up on the other side of the security checkpoint and had a cup of coffee while we joked about the obvious nonrandom selection.

"That didn't look very random, did it?" I asked with a smile as we sat down with our coffee.

"What would make you think that?" one of my brothers joked. "I don't see any similarities in the three of us."

"Perhaps this is a family thing," my other brother suggested with a chuckle. "They just don't like the Ganies flying."

"I think the real problem is that they just don't like the Ganies' ethnicity," I added.

We were early for our flights, since we all knew that looking the way we do post 9-11 meant that you needed to get to the airport long before the average Joe did, so my brothers decided they would go have a cigarette before our plane boarded. Because the entire SeaTac Airport is non-smoking, they would have to go out to the first level outside to get a quick cigarette in before we took off.

"I may as well join you," I said as they got up to head for the south end of the airport where the smokers congregated.

How I Became a Terrorist

Once we got outside, we decided we would give the secondary screening a second test; we wanted to turn our hypothesis into a theory by proving it over and over again.

"We'll just do the exact same thing again," I told my brothers as they puffed away on their cigarettes. "This time we'll just go in a different order, but we'll keep ten or so people between us."

"I can already tell you how this will end," one of my brothers said as he smashed his cigarette into the cigarette receptacle that was planted exactly 25 feet away from the airport entrance.

"I can too," I said. "I just want to prove myself right."

My brothers both finished their cigarettes and we headed back to the lines to pass through security for a second time that morning. Just as we planned, we stepped in line, letting a dozen or so people file in between us. To no one's surprise, we were all three stopped again "at random" to go through the secondary screenings. I almost chucked as I was being led to the side of the line. Once we had all made it through our second, secondary screenings, we discussed what had just taken place.

"What are the chances that three of us were selected for secondary screenings at the same airport twice within an hour?" I asked my brothers quietly as we sat in the waiting area for our flight to arrive.

"Well, I think it's safe to say that there is definitely nothing random about it," my older brother replied as he settled into his chair. "That didn't appear to be random in the least," he added.

Edan Ganie

"At least not to the three of us," my other brother commented.

"It's profiling," I said as my mouth grew into a frown. "They're stopping us based solely on how we look. It's not fair."

Later in 2012 I got to experience profiling at its best yet again when I was travelling from Miami back home to Seattle from a business trip. While I was in Miami, I had used a rental car to get to and from business meetings. The day of my flight back home, I had to return the car back to the airport car rental before I could check in. I got the car back without a problem, got my bags checked, and then went through security, where of course I was "randomly" selected to go through a secondary screening.

Once I received my pat down and the TSA employee handed me my carry-on, back, I made my way to my gate to sit and wait for my flight. I found an open seat and went to sit down, but as I reached into my pocket for my cell phone to make a quick call, I realized that my phone was nowhere to be found.

I stood for a moment and thought about where my phone could be. I searched my briefcase, then my carry-on, and then my pockets again. I thought about the security search. Had I seen my phone then? Did I leave it there? No, I hadn't had my phone then either. Then I realized I had left it in the rental car.

At that point I had to make a decision. I knew if I went back to get my phone, I was going to have to go through the whole routine again. I was afraid about the time it would take and wasn't terribly thrilled

How I Became a Terrorist

about all the stares I would receive once again while my belongings were searched, but I also needed my phone. I had all my contacts in it and I also always called my wife to check in while I travelled, and I didn't want her to worry. So, I finally came to the conclusion that I would have to bite the bullet and go to retrieve my phone.

Luckily for me, the rental company I had used was only about fifteen minute away from my terminal, but still I knew I was going to have to go through the rigmarole of security so I would have to hurry even if I wasn't far from the rental company.

I rushed to the car rental I had just left the car at and went right to the window where an employee was taking the keys. I explained my situation and thankfully the car hadn't even been moved yet. The man working grabbed the keys and led me over to the car. Inside on the console, there was my phone; right where I left it.

"Thank you so much," I said to the man as I grabbed my phone and then hurried off.

Because I was very aware of the screening process and how I always managed to fall on the TSA employees' radars when I passed by, when anything didn't go as planned, I couldn't help but get a little nervous because I, unlike the average non-Muslim flyer, could never just simply go through security. For me, there was no walking through the metal detector, gathering my wallet and change, and heading to my gate.

I heard people everywhere complaining about how they had to take their shoes off and what a pain it was to go through all the excessive security measures, while

Edan Ganie

I would have given anything to *only* have to go through the primary screening that so many people grumbled about. I realized that those checkpoints were in place for our benefit, and I had no qualms with them. What I did find bothersome, however, was the way I was always pulled out of line to undergo an additional process just because I was of Indian descent, especially if I had to go through it twice in a day. And it wasn't just the additional ten minutes that bothered me about these screenings; it was the way people looked at me as they passed and also the fact that I knew these selections were anything but random. I was being singled out because of my race and religion. In a sense, I was being vilified, and that is something that no one should have to feel any time they have to go on a business trip or want to take their families on vacation.

Needless to say, I was chosen for additional screening while coming back through from getting my phone. As soon as I saw a woman in a TSA uniform on the other side of the checkpoint, I looked down at my watch. I had less than half an hour to board. I shifted my weight and hoped that the woman would just let me by. I had already been through once, anyway, so I thought that perhaps she would remember that and let me go. No such luck.

I got to the front of the line and placed my bags on the conveyor belt to send them on their way through the scanner, removed my shoes, belt, and emptied the contents of my pockets in a little, light blue bowl and proceeded through the full-body scanner. I pulled in a breath and held it for a moment as I walked slowly

How I Became a Terrorist

through the scanner. As soon as I was on the other side, there she was.

"I need you to step aside, sir," the woman said as I reached for my belongings. "Is this your only bag?" she asked as she snatched my carry-on off the conveyor belt as soon as the scanner had spit it out.

"Yes ma'am," I told her as I turned to follow her.

I knew the routine well. She didn't have to tell me what to do next. I knew what all this meant. I heard the same monotone order dozens of times a year as I travelled around the United States for business. I probably knew the routine as well as all the agents by now.

"This way please, sir," she said as she made for the secondary screening area. Did she really not remember that I had just gone through all this less than an hour ago?

"I'm a bit short on time for my flight," I managed to say as the agent took me to secondary screening area and placed my bag on the table to search it.

"I don't care about your flight," she replied with a hard look. "I guess you should've left earlier," she added as she yanked the zipper of my bag open.

I was a little taken aback by the curt response of the woman and I remained quiet for the remainder of the procedure. I didn't make a sound as she searched my belongings, took swipes for GSR, a male TSA Agent came and I was patted down from head to toe. The additional procedures were never exactly pleasant, but this ranked as one of the tensest screenings I had ever endured. I felt as though the woman saw me as less than

Edan Ganie

human all of a sudden. When she was so rude about my concerns with missing my flight, I began to realize she didn't see me as a random person in an airport at all; she saw me as a potential threat and she didn't like me much because of it.

For fifteen silent and painfully awkward minutes I stood speechless while the agent finished going through all the steps. It was a long fifteen minutes that seemed to drag on into eternity. Between the harshness of the agent and the little time I had, it was also a strenuous fifteen minutes.

Even with the double secondary screening and the cell phone debacle, I did make my flight that day. The second run through the additional searches may not have caused me a delay in getting home, but it did convince me once and for all that the secondary screenings were not simple random searches.

The Miami airport was not the only run-in with obvious profiling I had in a Florida airport. I was travelling with my family (my wife, two sons and my daughter) on a family vacation and I experienced a similar situation, only this time it was at the Ft. Lauderdale airport, and this time my family was there to witness the whole thing.

For years, my family and I have been travelling to South Florida for family vacations. We have family and friends from Guyana scattered throughout the area, so South Florida has become a favorite getaway for us. We are able to fly down for short or lengthy visits and enjoy the Florida sun, warm, sandy beaches, and also visit with friends and loved ones.

How I Became a Terrorist

On one particular trip that we took, as our vacation was winding down and my family was preparing to return home by packing their suitcases and double-checking the hotel room to be sure that they didn't leave anything behind, I was mentally preparing myself for the airport. I was fully expecting to be chosen for yet another "random screening." There was something about being pulled away from my family that was particularly unnerving for me—more so than being picked out with my brothers or a colleague, though that was also quite embarrassing—so I needed a bit more time to get ready for the airport that day.

Finally the time came and we were off to the airport. We got our rental car checked in and our bags checked and headed for the checkpoint to get into the main terminal. We made it to the front of the line and one by one we hoisted our carry-ons to the conveyor belt and took off our shoes, belts, watches, etc. My daughter went through the metal detector, then my two sons, and my wife—my wife was selected for a private screening because she wears a headscarf—and finally, me. I waited for the agent, and like clockwork, there appeared in front of me a TSA uniform.

"I'm going to need you to step aside, sir," I heard.

Of the five travelling, I was the one chosen "at random" to go onto a secondary screening. I wasn't surprised in the least and neither was my family. They were so accustomed to it that they would stand off to the side out of the way of other passengers but still nearby and wait once they were out, knowing that I would be pulled aside for an extra ten or fifteen minutes.

Edan Ganie

By now I was convinced that I fit a certain profile that TSA used for selecting travelers to screen for further security. I noticed that I was always selected regardless of with whom I flew. It didn't matter whether I was travelling alone, with my family, or with business acquaintances; I was always the one chosen to step aside and have my belongings searched and swiped.

Knowing that every time I stepped foot in an airport I was going to be subject to these additional searches was an inconvenience at best and an injustice at worst. I was being singled out on purpose; that was clear. Why I was being singled out, beyond race, I did not know, however. I did know that this was a part of my life now, though, so if I wanted to continue to travel, I had better get used to it and try to let each incident go as they occurred, and I did my best to do just that.

As much as I was learning to tolerate the harassment for these TSA secondary screenings, however, I was not prepared for what was to come when I travelled for business internationally. I thought that having a TSA agent pat me down and go through my bags was a little maddening and unfair, but I had no idea how bad it would get. Travelling within the States had been tough, but the real trouble would come with every flight returning home from a foreign country. TSA was a cakewalk compared to what I would experience with immigration and customs.

CHAPTER ELEVEN:

Prove Your Patriotism or Leave

As my business ventures expanded internationally, I began travelling move frequently and to more countries where I had money invested. My very first international business had me visiting Asia on a regular basis; thus, my experience with airport security in Bangkok. My next international venture was vested in the Caribbean, more specifically in Trinidad and Tobago. After Trinidad, I set my eyes on my homeland, Guyana. With my new enterprises scattered about the globe, I practically lived in airports. I was also learning a valuable lesson about the difference between flying out of the States and coming back in. For a man who's been put on a kind of flying blacklist, the difference is great, and you will soon find out what I mean by that.

When travelling to Guyana, the most convenient route to get there was through the Port of Spain. From there I would make my way to Guyana, which was only a 45-minute flight. When I took an early flight, the short trip allowed me to get to Georgetown to conduct business for the entire day. After I concluded my business in Guyana, instead of staying overnight, I would head back to the airport and make my way back

Edan Ganie

home to Seattle. When you are always travelling, every extra minute at home is valuable, so I was grateful that I was able to get to and from Guyana so quickly.

On May 11, 2009, I was travelling via Continental Airline to Port of Spain, Trinidad; there was one stop along the way in Houston. After I arrived in Trinidad, I would have to switch airlines, however, because Continental Airlines did not fly into Guyana. From Trinidad I would use Caribbean Airlines to Guyana, then I would return to Seattle on Delta Airlines, so that meant that I would be hopping around from airline to airline for my May 11th trip, and the trip seemed cursed from the beginning. On my very first layover in Houston, I experienced something that I never had before—something that baffled me and that prepared me for things to come.

As I was waiting to board my flight from Houston to Trinidad, Port of Spain, I was sitting reading a book when I heard my name announced by the Continental Airlines boarding gate attendant.

"Edan Ganie, please come to the ticket counter," I heard the mechanical voice of the flight attendant say over the loudspeaker.

I stopped right where I was in my book and looked up. My heart skipped a beat the moment I heard my own name announced. I had no idea what was going on or why I was being summoned by the airlines. I was travelling business class, so I knew I was not on any upgrade list. With no other possible explanation, my mind instantly went to disaster and my family. Did something happen at home? Was there some

How I Became a Terrorist

emergency that I didn't know about yet? There was only one way to find out.

"Excuse me," I said to flight attendant behind the counter. "I am Edan Ganie. My name was just called."

Behind the woman stood four CBP officers with their arms all crossed over their chests; two were glancing around the terminal and two were staring at me.

"I've been told that Customs and Border Protection needs to see you," she said in the same voice she used to announce my name.

At that point the four officers' eyes were all on me. They stepped forward from behind the counter and took me aside to ask me a series of questions.

"What is the purpose of this trip, Mr. Ganie?" one officer asked, a man, a little over six feet tall and built like an old college football player.

"Business," I told him. "I am travelling to my home country of Guyana for business."

"What kind of business?" the stocky officer asked as the others stood silent and watched me carefully, as if I were a flight risk.

"It's mining supplies," I told him. "I have investments in mining in Guyana."

"Are you carrying more than $10,000 with you today, Mr. Ganie?" the same man asked. I assumed he was the ringleader since the others stood mute.

"No," I told him, confused by the last question. I couldn't imagine that one, there was any reason for anyone to travel with so much cash; and, two, why they would want to know or assume that I was.

97

Edan Ganie

After the questioning was over, it was time for the searching. Finally the other three had something to do other than look intimidating. They all searched my bag, my wallet and all my other personal items. This I was more accustomed to. It was like my usual secondary screenings.

"You can board the plane now," the ringleader told me once they had gone through all my belongings.

They failed to tell me why exactly they had pulled me aside and the reason for all the questions. I could tell though that my questions wouldn't get me very far so I didn't even try to ask. As I gathered my things, I noticed that my head felt a little heavier than usual and that my skin a little hotter. It was the feeling of shock and humiliation. Being pulled aside, questioned, and searched in front of all my fellow passengers was by far the most humiliating moment in all my travels!

I had been through countless TSA screenings by that time, and none of them came close to degrading me the way this experience had. My name was announced aloud and I had to walk up to the counter in front of hundreds of passengers whose eyes were glued to me the entire way; it felt like dead man's walk. And what's more, I was the only one called for this screening. Of the hundreds of others sitting in the terminal that day, I was the sole passenger called out.

Still shaken up by the incident, I took my seat. As I hoisted my bag over my head to get it in the overhead compartment, I couldn't stop thinking about what had just happened. I sat down to read my book, but all I could do was replay the event in my head. I could only

How I Became a Terrorist

come up with one conclusion for the way I was treated that day; I was undoubtedly being profiled by the U.S. Authorities. Not just me as a male of Indian descent who looked to be Muslim, but me as individual. They called my name that day, Edan Ganie. It was more than just being picked on because my skin color now. I was on a list of some kind and I hadn't a clue how or why.

Not too long after that incident I travelled again to the Caribbean, Trinidad and Guyana, to conduct some business. This time I made a stop in Miami to meet with some colleagues for investment undertakings I had in South Florida. Once I was finished with my meetings in Florida, I left Miami for Port of Spain. I didn't know what to expect after my last flight to the Caribbean, but the trip into Trinidad seemed to go smoothly, comparatively speaking.

A few days after I arrived in Trinidad I travelled to Guyana to meet with my attorney, who is general counsel for my Caribbean ventures. Again, there were no unusual dealings that took place as I travelled to and from Guyana, so I thought that this time my trip wouldn't be so eventful as the last. Perhaps I could escape a business trip without harassment. My optimism was premature.

I flew into Miami on Caribbean Airlines and as soon as I was off the plane, I was met by two CBP officers. They had my passport picture with my identity and they were waiting just for me.

"Mr. Ganie," one lanky man said as I took my first step onto the carpet of the airport terminal. "I'm Officer

Edan Ganie

Malone with Customs and Border Protection. I'm going to need your passport please. And follow me."

They took my passport and customs form and escorted me through the immigration line. With one CBP officer in front of me and the other behind me, I was ushered to the front of the line past hundreds of people who stood watching the way spectators watch a criminal being marched into the courtroom on the day of a trial. I may as well have been wearing an orange jumpsuit and handcuffs. I was mortified.

Each time that this happened seemed to be getting worse. The badgering had escalated from secondary screenings, to CBP officer shakedowns, and now I was being escorted around like a high-risk inmate. It wasn't just the ideas that I knew the strangers had about me that was so devastating this time, though; there were people on the flight who knew me—people I did business with and had known for years who were watching me led away by uniformed men. To everyone who could see the spectacle, I looked like I was some sort of wanted criminal being arrested. Yet no one offered any explanation as to why I was subjected to the humiliation and interrogations. The most I had received was an officer's name and the fact that they needed my information, but they never provided me with any details of their own.

After the CBP officers walked me through immigration they took me to a secure room where they interrogated me for four hours. The two officers were Tyson and Moss. Tyson questioned me about my trip

How I Became a Terrorist

while Officer Moss took the lead and searched my bags and personal items.

"Who did you meet with while you were in Trinidad?" Tyson asked.

"With my business associates," I told them. "I have businesses in Trinidad and Guyana and I meet with my lawyers and partners to discuss our investments."

"Who else did you talk to? It wasn't all business was it?"

"I really only know business associates in Trinidad," I explained. "So that is all I do while I am there."

"And you went to Guyana too," Tyson said. "What was your reason for that trip?"

I wondered for a moment why anyone would ask why someone would return to their homeland. When people travel home for the holidays, do they have to explain why? When a grandmother flies over to see her grandchildren who have moved to another country, do they have to explain themselves?

"I am from Guyana," I said, "but I also have a mining supply business there."

"And who did you talk to while you were there?"

"To my lawyer," I told them. "My lawyer for my Caribbean ventures is in Georgetown, so I visited him to discuss all my investments."

"Guyana is where you were born, so I assume you talked to others while you were there besides your lawyer. Who else did you speak to in Guyana?" Tyson demanded.

I answered each question as it came, all the while absolutely ignorant as to why I was being grilled about

101

Edan Ganie

everything I did and everyone I came into contact with. Officer Tyson questioned my business ventures. He wanted to know how many companies I invested in and about the business financials. He also wanted to know my personal tax return information.

"That information could easily be retrieved from the IRS," I explained when he asked about my tax information.

"I'm not asking the IRS for them. I'm asking *you*," he spat, red-faced. "And I am not asking you; I am telling you."

I could tell that Officer Tyson had a little bit of a temper and I didn't want to push my luck, so I tried my best to comply.

"These are enormous sets of financials," I explained, trying to tiptoe around his anger, "It will be a lot of paper, but I will mail them after I return home."

"I'm not messing around here, Mr. Ganie," Tyson snapped. He must have thought that I was getting smart with him. "You get me that information and you get it to me ASAP or you won't be doing anymore travelling. I'll sit here all day and night if I have to."

"I cannot remember the details of my various companies," I told him once I realized that he had no intentions of letting me leave until I regurgitated mountains of financial information I had no way of knowing. "Everything is handled by my CPA, but I can give you an overview," I offered, trying to do what I could to appease him and avoid another temper flare.

"Just give me an estimation then," he barked.

How I Became a Terrorist

"I receive a Schedule K-1 for each of my ventures in each company," I explained. "These are included in my Schedule 1040 for my personal taxes."

As I tried to explain my financial information, Tyson knitted his brows and clenched his teeth. He seemed perplexed by everything I was trying to explain. I was sure that he didn't understand what I was talking about. You almost needed to be a CPA to grasp it, so I didn't understand why he was pushing so hard for it in the first place.

Officer Tyson was obviously outside his comfort zone, so he shifted the conversation to get back to something he was familiar with so he could prove to me how smart he was. I knew that he wanted to show me he was still in control.

"I spent years serving my country in the service. I was highly trained by the military and did a tour in Iraq to serve my country," he boasted with his fisted hands glued to the table. "I am a patriot for my country and I proved it with my service," he said, I assumed to suggest that I was not.

"I think we are all serving our country in various ways," I replied in response to his implication that I hadn't done my job as an American.

Officer Tyson shifted in his seat as he crossed his arms over his chest. He didn't have a response so I went on.

"I also contribute to this beautiful country of ours. I am an entrepreneur; I create jobs. I provide employment for about 100 people in the US," I said proudly, standing my ground. "My business not only creates employment,

Edan Ganie

but I also pay taxes to the federal government, state and local government."

"I did more than just pay taxes," he snorted. "I fought for my country."

"I serve our country in that my taxes help pay the military budget," I replied, and added, "My taxes also pay your agency's budget, including your position."

"Are you willing to serve your country?" Tyson snarled.

"What do you mean? I just said we all serve in various ways."

"Are you willing to die for your country?"

"No," I said with force. "I am in my fifties and contribute to my community in multiple ways. I don't feel I need to fight and die at this age."

"If you are not willing to die for your country, you should not live in the US," he spat, his finger pointing and the vessels in his head throbbing. I sat and didn't say a word. I could not believe what I was hearing.

"Are you a Sunni Muslim?" he asked when I didn't have a response to his misguided patriotism.

The entire interview had been appalling and, dare I say, unconstitutional, but this question floored me. He had crossed every line one could outside of becoming physically violent at that point, and I would not be harassed any further by this ignorant racist.

"What does it matter to the US authorities if I am a Sunni Muslim?" I asked with venom in my words. "Do you even know the difference between a Sunni Muslim from the other denominations?"

"It doesn't matter to me what God you pray to," Tyson blurted. He met my anger with more anger.

How I Became a Terrorist

By the time we hit our heated climax in which Tyson proved to me he knew nothing about Muslims what-so-ever, the interrogation had been going on for about three hours. Tyson was taking lead and the other officer was in and out of the room. They emptied my bag, searched everything, and even took my wallet and copied my credit cards. They took my cell phone and downloaded all the information from it. They copied all my business papers then gave me a personal pat down.

"You'll have to wait now," Tyson said as he made for the door. "We have to make a call to our superiors for permission to release you."

About forty-five minutes later a superior returned the phone call and granted permission for my release. I was escorted through the baggage and customs area to make sure I had no other bags there. Then I was told that I was free to go.

That was the first time I had experienced such an intense and completely berating and inappropriate shakedown during my travels, but it would not be the last. I experienced fifteen such experiences over the past two years travelling internationally for business and vacations. In the Miami international airport alone I have gone through similar embarrassing interrogations at least three times.

CHAPTER TWELVE:

Are You Waiting for Me?

Shortly after Tyson's shakedown, I returned from a trip to the Caribbean to Miami. Again, I was met at the plane door by two CBP officers. This time I was ready. I approached them with my passport in-hand and asked, "Are you waiting for me?"

"How did you know?" one asked. I could see they were both surprised.

"I was expecting you," I said.

They escorted me through immigration past the crowd. Just as before, everyone was looking at me like a criminal being taken away after sentencing. I was taken to another small room where I was told to sit and wait while the CBP officers got all my information to their supervisor, who was sitting right in front of me on the opposite side of a glass partition. One of the officers handed the supervisor all my information and I watched as she took my passport and placed it on her desk. With that the supervisor got up from her desk, grabbed her lunch box, and left with two other CBP officers for lunch. I watched the three women head off for their break and then I waited, and waited, and waited.

Edan Ganie

An hour passed and I figured that soon someone would be coming back in from lunch. I was a little shocked that they would just leave me there for that hour, but I figured once the break was over someone would be back to question me and let me go.

I saw officers come and go in the tiny room the supervisor had left my information in, and each time I would hope that one or two of them would grab my paperwork and come into the room I was in, but each time they came and went without even glancing in my direction. I counted fourteen officers total who simply ignored my presence altogether. Perhaps they were all on lunch, I thought. Once the hour was over, surely one of them would come in.

But then another thirty minutes went by and not a single person came in to tell me anything. I sat, getting more frustrated by the minute. As I sat alone in the room, I observed officers strolling by chatting. I heard them in the next room discussing personal affairs while I sat and waited. I heard them talking about their vacations to Puerto Rico, refinancing their home loans, how much money they saved and what they were planning to do with it.

As I sat and stared at my watch, I listened to mindless chatter, but no one thought to come in and tell me what was going on or when I could leave. One of the men spent quite some time talking about his son's boxing. He was telling four other officers how his son would be going to regionals if he won his next fight. After that the conversation branched out to other subjects like jogging in the park and the way some

How I Became a Terrorist

women's legs look like broomsticks. They spoke of the school system and how ineffective it was, but no one talked about the man they were holding in the next room. When another half hour had passed, putting me at two hours in a room with no human contact, I finally worked up the nerve to go to the desk and ask someone what was going on.

"Who is in charge here?" I asked the CBP officer behind the counter. "I have been sitting in there for two hours and no one has come in to tell me anything."

"My supervisor is gone for the day," the young woman said without apology. I could not believe how unprofessional the entire office was conducting itself.

Shortly after I spoke to the curt officer at the counter, I saw a senior CBP officer enter the room. I jumped at the chance to approach him.

"Excuse me, sir," I said as I walked toward the middle-age officer with graying hair and a mousy mustache. "I have been here for over two and a half hours and no one is helping me."

"I'm the supervisor for another section," he cut me off. "I'm only passing through. I'll call for someone to process you. This section has no one trained to process you."

About twenty minutes later two CBP officers came and took me to a secure room and began to question me about my trip—where I travelled, what business I conducted, who I met and spoke with on my trip. They searched my bags, briefcase, and wallet and in about half an hour made a phone call to their superiors.

Edan Ganie

"Why do you all have to make that call every time?" I asked one of the officers.

"It's called a "CYA" call," the officer told me. "'Cover your ass'. We don't have the authority to release you, so we have to get someone else to give the go-ahead."

Florida is not the only place this happens to me, however. I have experienced similar embarrassment several times at Houston International Airport. On one trip, two CBP officers met me at the ramp as I exited the plane. They took me through much of the same routine that the Miami officers did, but in Houston I noticed a profound difference.

The same CBP officer who processed me the first time I was stopped in Houston was the one to process me again. We remembered each other. The first time he processed me he spoke of his visit to Bremerton, Washington, and how he liked the community, so he obviously remembered everything about our last meeting.

Interestingly, he went through the same routine of questioning and searching my briefcase, bags, cell phone, and wallet again. The only difference was this time he received a return callback from his regional commander much quicker than the time before. I was processed in about three hours instead of the prior four hours.

Sometimes I re-enter the U.S. via New York's JFK Airport when I travel with Delta. At least three times I have been met at the door by CBP officers waiting with my photo. As instinctively as many begin to empty out their pockets when going through airport security, I

How I Became a Terrorist

have begun to look for and approach the CBP officers when I land back in the US. Each time I go straight to them and ask, "Are you waiting for me?" I always like the look of surprise on their faces when I do this.

Each time it is the same no matter what state I am in, too. There are two officers that walk me past the immigrations line, one in front of me and another behind me, as if I am being arrested and could bolt at any moment. In the beginning it made me feel nauseated to think of the way all the other passengers must have seen me, as a terrorist being taken into custody. I am now almost accustomed to such embarrassment and humiliation.

After the three to four hours of interrogation at JFK, one of the CBP officers always takes my cell phone and leaves the immigration area to download my contacts and other data. This always seems to take about an hour. After I have received all my belongings, I have to wait for the call from the regional commander to clear me to get on my flight back home. I am expected to undergo the same routine every time I travel.

I have come to expect and always plan for about a four hour delay for my connecting flight when returning home from my international trips. I cannot help but assume that the US authorities have designed the system for passengers who fit a certain profile to be detained, interrogated, and harassed when travelling. I cannot imagine that with today's technology and information sharing systems that once an individual is thoroughly processed at JFK, Houston or Miami, that

111

Edan Ganie

the information cannot be ascertained by CBP without the need of a four hour interrogation every time.

Even more intriguing is that when I am processed at one airport that I have to be subjected to the same set of repetitive questions again and again each time I return. Perhaps in a third world country without the technology, the constant interrogations would make sense, but not in a country like the United States with the technology the US authorities possess—unless the system is designed to harass specific travelers who have certain traits.

———

CHAPTER THIRTEEN:

By Land and Air, Harassment is There

British Columbia, Canada, is a favorite travel destination for my family and me. We make frequent trips up there for short getaways and enjoy the city, with all its sites and attractions. My sons and daughter are particularly fond of the restaurants there, as BC has a host of eateries that serve kosher food, which can be hard to come by in the United States. Along with loving the city itself, we have several friends and relatives in the area with whom we always love to visit. Every trip to Canada for us is filled with good company, good food, and a good Cuban cigar for me. It is a pleasure that we all look forward to throughout the year. The last few years, however, those lovely getaways have been plagued with an unpleasant grand finale.

For years I had been travelling with my family to and from Canada. Being in Washington, Canada is not too far a drive, but we still feel like we are in a whole other world once we arrive, so it really is an ideal getaway spot. Three-day weekends and short holidays is all the time we need to make a quick trip, but the years following the 9-11 attacks brought with them

Edan Ganie

a new obstacle for any Muslim who simply wishes to take a trip across any border with their families. Little by little, I was seeing just how far these obstacles could go and how much they could affect.

In July 2011, my family and I were returning home from a weekend in Vancouver and entered the US at the Blaine border crossing. We had passed through this checkpoint countless times without incident, so we thought nothing of it when we pulled up to the area. It was around half past six in the evening as we arrived at the border, and my two sons and ten-year-old daughter presented our passports to the CBP officer who stood behind a Plexiglas barrier that separated him from the travelers. Instead of being okayed to cross as we usually had been, we were then given a slip by the officer.

"Take this to the Customs Building," he said as he handed the slip back with our passports. "It's for secondary screening."

I can't even travel on the ground anymore, I thought as I gathered my children and headed for the Customs Building. It had been a hard pill to swallow to come to terms with the fact that I would never be able to fly overseas without hours of interrogation upon returning, but now my own children were being dragged into this mess, and my heart sunk as I thought about an officer talking to them the way that so many had spoken to me, with apathy at best and disdain at worst. I just hoped that since we were Washington residents and I had relatives in Canada, we wouldn't be subjected to the intense interrogations I always had been when flying.

How I Became a Terrorist

We found our way to the Customs Building and looked around for the counter to which we needed to present our little slips. I spotted it and led my sons and daughter over to the line; it wasn't a long one and it looked just the way I imagined it would, which was to say that there weren't many blond-headed, fair-skinned travelers in the line with my family and me.

We got to the front of the line and handed our slips over to the officer. He was a chubby guy with rust colored hair and a bushy mustache that made me want to scratch my own upper lip. He had tiny, little eyes and a bulbous nose that dwarfed the rest of his features. For having such strange features, though, he had a very bland personality.

"Have a seat," he finally told us after taking his time looking over the slips and our passports.

We all stood there looking around as the plump officer said this because, as far as we could all see, there were no seats anywhere in the vicinity to have. I didn't know if he didn't realize this or just didn't care too much, but there wasn't a chair in the place for any of us.

Three times I scanned the room to look for chairs and then looked at the chubby officer, but it was a lost cause. He offered no explanation and no seats, so I decided to search the room for something that would suffice. I saw some long, boxy, metal air vents that lined one of the walls about fifty feet from where we were standing.

"We'll just go sit over there," I said as I nodded my head toward the vents. "It looks like that's our best option."

Edan Ganie

My children and I scooted ourselves on the vents. They didn't seem terribly sturdy, so we leaned on them more than we sat on them. They were cold and dingy, so I hoped that we wouldn't be stuck there for too long.

"What are we doing?" my daughter asked.

"Waiting," I told her.

"Waiting for what?" she pushed.

"Waiting for someone to come and do a search so we can go on home."

"Why?" she asked me.

Why indeed, I thought as I looked down at my daughter. She was small enough that she could sit all the way on the vent, so she sat there, her eyes searching the place and her little legs swinging, one and then the other, as she looked around.

"It's just for security since we are crossing a border," I told her.

"We've never had to do this before," my oldest son piped in.

"We've been lucky then," I said. "It shouldn't take long."

"Good, because I'm starving," my son said as he shifted his weight. "We haven't had dinner yet."

"We'll get something as soon as we're done here," I promised. "It won't be long. They'll just look through our bags and let us go."

About fifteen minutes later we were approached by a CBP officer we had not yet seen that day. He had thinning silver hair and it was easy to see that his sense of urgency had dwindled away with his hairline. His nametag read "Emerson" on it. His wrinkled hands,

How I Became a Terrorist

covered with liver spots and rough with age, slowly took our passports and brought them up to eye level so his eyes could verify what his hands were holding. He took long, hard breaths as he did everything, which made the smallest movements seem like an arduous chore. I was exhausted just watching him.

"I'm gonna need to interview you," the elderly officer said to me. "I'll be right back."

Emerson turned and scooted away from us. I watched him as he walked away for a moment, his head dropping a little so that it looked like it was being propped up by his jutting shoulders. He slouched a little as he shuffled along and it looked like it took all he had to pick his feet up from the floor to get him from one place to the next. *This may take longer than usual*, I thought as I watched the old man.

After my many experiences with CBP officers in airports, I had no idea how long Emerson would really be gone. I'd been left in rooms for hours before without a single word, so I got a little nervous when I saw him shuffle away. Luckily though, he returned five minutes later. I knew the kids were getting hungrier by the minute and that my wife was waiting on us to return, so I was hoping we could move through all this as quickly as possible.

"You all can just wait here," he wheezed at the children. "I just need to interview your dad."

I could see panic flash in my daughter's eyes when the officer said this. My sons looked a little confused, but my daughter was obviously frightened.

Edan Ganie

"I'll be right back," I told them. "Just stay right here and I'll be back in no time."

I was taken to a secure room that looked a lot like all those interrogation rooms that you see in detective shows: four, drab concrete walls that had in them only a small metal desk and two metal chairs. The looks of the place made me think that at anytime they might turn a spotlight on me and start drilling me.

Another officer had joined us by this time. I sat in one of the chairs, Officer Emerson in the other, and the second officer stood beside me. I was beginning to feel like this was going to be yet another shakedown. I imagined with the two of them there, this would be a good cop-bad cop kind of thing, and I was willing to bet Mr. Emerson was too old and tired to play the bad cop.

"What was your reason for visiting British Columbia" Officer Emerson started.

"I went with my family for a weekend trip," I told him.

"Who did you visit while you were there?" he asked.

"My nephew lives there, so we visited him," I explained.

"And what is your nephew's name?"

I told the officers my nephew's name, and then Emerson wanted to know his home address, which I also provided.

"Do you have your social security card with you today?" Emerson asked after he gathered all my nephew's information.

How I Became a Terrorist

"I may," I said as I pulled my wallet out and began to search. I looked through my credit cards and business cards, but could not find my social security card. "I guess I don't have it," I told them as I was still holding my wallet in my hand.

"Do you know your social security number?"

"Yes," I said, and gave them the number.

While I was rummaging around in my wallet looking for my social security card, Mr. Emerson noticed that I had a concealed weapon permit and a pilot license.

"What kind of planes do you fly?" he prodded when he saw the license. I told him what kind of planes and the airport that I generally used.

"Why do you carry a concealed weapons permit?"

"So I can carry a handgun," I answered. Isn't that why anyone carried a concealed weapons permit?

"Why do you need a handgun?" he went on.

"For protection."

"Do you have a concealed weapon with you today?"

"No, I don't travel with a handgun," I told him. When I knew I'd be traveling across borders, I always thought it was best not to bring my handgun, so I had been in the habit of leaving my gun at home when I traveled to Canada.

"I'm going to need you to stand up and put your hands against the wall," Emerson said.

If I hadn't been so accustomed to these searches and violations of privacy, I may have been shocked by this. Since I'd been patted down and questioned so many times before though, I just went along with everything without saying a word.

119

Edan Ganie

I stood up and faced the concrete wall. I pressed my palms into the cold, bumpy surface and stood there as the other officer frisked me. Once he was finished, the officer stepped back and grunted, "Okay."

I sat back in the metal chair and watched as Officer Emerson took both my pilot license and my concealed weapons permit to make copies of them. Again, I sat silent. Even though I had gone through every legal avenue I was asked to get both of those, I sat quietly and answered all the questions I was asked. Even though I knew that the United States and/or the State of Washington was already well aware that I had both since I had taken classes and provided all my personal information to get them, I stayed completely quiet. I knew that there was no reason for this additional questioning and that a thousand other people who didn't have dark skin or an accent could have walked through with those pieces of paper in their wallets and no one would bat an eye, but I kept silent and complied to whatever I was told because all I wanted to do was to get back to my kids and get on with my life.

CHAPTER FOURTEEN:

More Money, More Problems

"How much money do you have in your wallet right now?" Officer Emerson asked once they had copied of my license and permit.

I took my wallet and opened it up to where I kept my bills and started to count it as they watched. "100, 200, 300…" I counted as their eyes zeroed in on my hands. The total was $1,600.

"Why do you have so much cash on hand" Officer Emerson asked while his silent partner just raised an eyebrow. "That's an awful lot of cash to be walking around with."

"I like to take enough cash to use during my vacation," I explained. "When I go to British Columbia, I just bring enough so that I won't have to use my debit or credit cards."

"I don't care if I'm on a vacation or not," Emerson scoffed, "I never carry that kind of cash around on me and I don't think it's a very good idea that you do either. No one needs that kind of cash for a weekend."

Emerson and his partner had been pretty intrusive throughout the process, but I knew that they were asking a series of stock questions, so I kept silent, even

Edan Ganie

if I did think it was ridiculous that I had to answer them. He had gone from asking questions to making personal commentary, though, and I was getting to my wit's end. Besides that, it had been a half hour now and my children were sitting by themselves starving on the other side of the door.

"Is having 1,600 dollars illegal?" I snapped, fed up with the entire process.

"No, "he said, "it's not illegal, but it isn't very smart and it also looks pretty suspicious. I just can't see any reason what-so-ever to carry around that much money. That's what banks are for. I only know a few kinds of people who need to deal in cash, and I don't think you want to be associated with any of them," he lectured.

As the old officer sat with his palms pressed to the table and instructed me on how I should conduct myself where money was concerned, I decided it was best not to say anything else. He asked me a series of questions after this, and I gave short, simple answers just to avoid another harangue. Once he felt he had asked me everything he could, I was taken back to the room with my children. It was half past seven by this time.

As I rejoined my children Mr. Emerson handed one of my sons, his wallet, which was a shock to all of us because we didn't know they even had the wallet. Apparently our vehicle had been searched while I was being interviewed and it was taken at that time. I had no idea that our car would be searched and I was a little stunned when I learned this fact.

How I Became a Terrorist

"Count your money just to make sure it's all there," Emerson said as he stared at my son.

"It's all there," my son said after he counted. "2,200 dollars is what I came with."

"If I had your money, I would just burn mine," Emerson remarked in a snarky tone.

"What does that mean?" I asked the critical old man.

"Where did the boy get so much cash?" Emerson shot back.

"I spent the summer working, cleaning my dad's office building, our apartment building, and the parking lot to make the money," my son answered.

By the time that the officers were finished with me, finished searching the car, and finished lecturing my family, it was after 10p.m. and no one had eaten anything since lunch. My sons were older and more understanding and patient. However, my 10-year-old daughter was hungry and irritated.

Although I had tried to explain to her what we were doing there, she didn't fully understand why the CBP were conducting secondary security screenings or what it all meant. She was hungry and tired and that was her only concern, and rightfully so for a child. No ten-year-old should be kept in a cold, uncomfortable building without seats or anything to eat or drink for hours when they were just trying to get back home from a short vacation.

That wasn't the end of the experience, either. The officers gave us our belongings back, but we were left waiting on the air vents once again. For two more hours we shifted, stood, leaned, and sat as we waited

123

Edan Ganie

for someone to let us go. We had been there for almost six hours at that point, without a chair or a bite to eat. My daughter was hungry and tired, and she asked every fifteen minutes, "Can we leave now, dad? I'm so hungry."

It got to be near midnight and we noticed the CBP officers were changing shifts. At just about ten minutes to midnight, Mr. Emerson noticed that my daughter was crying to me about how hungry she was.

"Could we get her something to eat, please?" I asked him. "There's not a vending machine or even a water fountain and we've been here almost six hours."

At that, Emerson grumbled something under his breath. I didn't know what he said, but I could tell by his expression and the fact that he didn't just come out and say it that it wasn't a nicety.

"Pardon me?" I said to him. "I didn't hear what you said." Emerson just turned and walked away.

I was on the brink of an outburst by this time. Treating me poorly was one thing, but questioning my son and ignoring my daughter's hunger was more than I could stand for. I marched to the counters and asked one of the CBP officers if I could speak with the supervisor. The officer pointed to a desk, so I followed where his finger directed me and introduced myself to the officer.

"My name is Edan Ganie," I told him. "I have been here since about 6:30 and I was just wondering if someone could help us."

"Hello, Mr. Ganie. I'm Officer Gatis," the man said as he looked over at my family. "What can I do for you?"

How I Became a Terrorist

"My daughter is very hungry but there is nothing here to eat. I tried to tell Mr. Emerson about it, but he just mumbled and walked away," I explained.

"I apologize about that," Gatis said, sympathetic to our situation. "Mr. Emerson should have allowed you all to arrange for something to eat. We have some snacks for the children."

By then, Mr. Emerson was walking towards us with his backpack ready to leave. He told us we were free to go. We could have been upset about the wait and the way Emerson treated us, but we were thrilled to finally be set free from that place. We hurried out of the Customs Building and found the closest restaurant that was open.

Before we left the building, I told Mr. Gatis that I would like to file a complaint. He gave me some pamphlets about CBP policies and a form for feedback about how we were treated. The form consisted of a questionnaire that merely asked a question and provided for a fill in the blank response: fair, poor, or excellent.

"I need to write my comments," I told Mr. Gatis as I looked over the form.

"That's really all we have," he told me.

That following week I called Congressman Adam Smith's officer and shared my horrible experience. I spoke with Ruth, a compassionate and warm staff member who seemed to really care about what had happened, and then followed up with emails to her. I also spoke wit her about my other travel experiences when I would return to the US from my business trips. She was beyond sympathetic and promised to help,

125

Edan Ganie

so I emailed her all the details and she did speak with the CBP.

Some months later, Ruth called me and said that she attended a meeting with CBP and other agencies. CBP personnel denied that the waiting area had no chairs.

CHAPTER FIFTEEN:

I Must Interrogate You but I Don't Know What Questions to Ask

In June 2011, I was on a business trip to the Caribbean. I travelled first to Guyana, and then to Trinidad, where I met with a couple of attorneys to discuss a business case. We had meetings to mediate a settlement with a judge at the Hall of Justice in Port of Spain. I would then return to Guyana after a few days to visit with family and friends.

The flight out of the United States didn't seem to cause too much trouble, but when I was leaving Guyana, I came head-to-head with yet another obstacle for reasons unbeknownst to me.

The morning that I was to fly out of Guyana, I checked my flight to make sure everything was running on time and then had a cup of coffee at the airline lounge. At that point, everything seemed normal enough. I finished my coffee and went on to board the plane. I was flying with a business associate on this trip, so we settled into our seats and started talking business. As we were in the middle of our conversation, a flight attendant approached us.

Edan Ganie

"Are you Mr. Ganie?" she said softly as she leaned over so that our eyes would meet.

"Yes I am," I told her. I could feel the blood start to rush to my face. *Not with a business partner here*, I thought.

"Can you bring your bag and come with me?" It was an order, not a request.

I complied. She took me back to the boarding area and I could feel the weight of a hundred set of eyes pounding down onto me as we passed. It was no easier this time than it had been the first. I could feel my palms getting damp and the blood that had made its way to the surface of my skin was tingling just below the surface. I could hardly breathe I was so humiliated. I was going to have to sit back down and fly with all these people after this, who assumed God knew what about me. It was a nightmare.

At the boarding area, two airport security personnel and airline security personnel were waiting.

"Did you check any bags," a burly man asked as he took my carry-on from my hands.

"No," I told them. "I didn't travel with checked bags."

With that, they unzipped the only bag I had and emptied everything out of it. My slacks, socks, books, and undergarments lay strung out before me. It seems like such a small thing, but there is a sense of violation that comes with having all your personal belongings dumped out in front of a small crowd. I felt embarrassed and a little exposed, even if I had experienced this a thousand times before in the secondary searches

How I Became a Terrorist

because this time there were more people present and we were not at a security checkpoint.

After searching my bag and swiping it for gun shot residue, they told me I could re-board the plane. I did, but by this time the departure time had past and the flight was late. I could only assume it was because of me. I felt like I needed to apologize to everyone on the plane, but then again I had no idea what I would have been apologizing for.

I boarded the plane once again, and this time I was humiliated. I tried to ignore all the stares as I made my way to my seat. I placed my bag in the overhead bin and sat down as quickly as I could. I wanted to absorb into the tweed cushions of the seat so I wouldn't have to face the strangers or my business partner after that.

As I tried to push the event out of my mind, I could hear the whispers from passengers sitting around me on the plane. I couldn't make out any distinct words, but I knew that the whispers were about what took just place. I imagined that people were discussing whether or not I was a terrorist or becoming silently nervous as I re-boarded the plane, worried that I might cause a problem since I had been asked to leave.

"What was that about?" my colleague asked as I slouched in my seat.

"I have no idea," I told him. "If that happens, it is usually at the security checkpoints."

"Did they not say anything to you about why they were doing that?"

"Not a word," I told him. "They never do, though."

129

Edan Ganie

Neither I nor my colleague had any guess as to why I had been taken off the plane and searched once again. I would soon find out, however, when the plane landed.

When I returned to Guyana from my meetings in Trinidad, an even more interesting, if you could call it that, event took place at the Guyana airport. I cleared Immigration and Customs at the Cheddi Jagan International Airport and proceeded to the exit through the crowd, which stood waiting for their just-arrived relatives and friends. I met my driver on the other side of the gate and we were having a cup of coffee at a coffee shop right outside the airport's exit. Because the coffee shop is so near the exit, the area is always packed with people who are waiting to pick up travelers coming in from other destinations.

As we were sipping our coffee, my driver and I were approached by a young female immigration officer, the same one who had stamped my passport. Her voice shook a little when she talked and she seemed very shifty as she approached us. I could see she was very nervous.

"May I have your passport, please?" she asked me as her eyes darted around the crowd.

"What's going on?" I asked as I was reaching in my coat pocket for my passport.

"I just need you to follow me back to Immigration please, Mr. Ganie," she said, avoiding my question. She seemed like she was winded as she spoke to me. I thought it was strange that she was the nervous one when I was the one being pulled away from my coffee by an Immigration officer.

How I Became a Terrorist

I was upset by the lack of information and a little irritated after having been humiliated on my last flight, but I cooperated and went with the woman back to Immigration. When we made it inside the immigration area, we went into a room that immigration and customs used to interview passengers. Two other officers, one police detective and a senior immigration officer, joined the young woman at that point. This was getting out of hand.

"What is going on?" I insisted as the two other officers approached.

"We were requested to interview you and search your bag, Mr. Ganie," the senior officer explained.

"I want to know why," I said firmly. "And I want to have my attorney present for this. Someone needs to tell me what this is about."

They agreed to let me call my attorney, which I did immediately. I explained to him that I'd been pulled off my last flight and now I was being held at Immigration by three officers. I also told him that I'd already been cleared, but then a woman sought me out in a coffee shop and made me follow her back to be questioned.

"Just sit tight," my attorney told me. "I'm going to call the deputy immigration commissioner and find out what this is about."

I waited there with the three officers while calls were made so someone could explain to me why I was being harassed and humiliated all day as I travelled. Once all the appropriate channels were contacted, the senior officer stepped up to tell me what was going on.

131

Edan Ganie

"What is happening is that the U.S. authorities have requested, through the Joint Regional Communication Center for the Caribbean countries in Barbados, to put you on a watch list. That is why we had to pull you in for the interview," the officer told me.

"What do you need to know?" I asked, perplexed by the entire thing.

"Unfortunately, we don't really know what questions to ask you," the senior officer said. "We just know that we are required to interrogate you, but they don't tell us what to ask."

They verified my identity and then they searched my bag. After that was all finished, the senior officer apologized for the inconvenience and let me go. I tried not to be angry with them, as they were simply following orders, but I could not help to be irritated with the system in general. I had been put on some list, but I had no idea why or when or how I could get myself off it. I am a US citizen who had never been in any kind of trouble in my life. I am a businessman who had worked my way up from a bag boy at a military grocery store. My own brother served in the US military for years. I had done absolutely nothing to rouse suspicion in anyone and I wanted some real answers, but I've found that answers are not easy to come by when the government is involved.

Just two moths after that incident, I was travelling back to Guyana for business. When I stepped off the plane I headed to Immigration, as usual. Once I got to the front of the line, I handed my passport to the officer to get my stamp and go on about my day.

How I Became a Terrorist

"I am going to need you to step aside and wait please, Mr. Ganie," the young woman said from behind the counter.

"Why?" I asked her.

"I need to get my supervisor before you can pass," she explained. I stepped aside and waited.

When the supervisor came about ten minutes later, she called a custom's officer. They took me into the same room I had been taken to for questioning on my prior trip. Once again, I felt the intense heat of embarrassment work its way through my body as I had to stand aside and wait while every other passenger came and went through the line. Each person who passed through the line glanced over at me as they came to the counter to show their passports and receive their stamps. I knew just what was going through their minds as they stole glances at the man being held at Immigration.

During the interview, the same police detective from my previous trip entered the room. It took him no time to explain to the immigration supervisor that the US had requested JRCC to question my travels. This interview was a brief one because everyone in the room realized that the request was without merit. The officers had no idea what to do, so all they could do was send me on my way. Like me, they were at a loss as to why I was there and what the purpose of the interrogation was. Unlike me though, they wouldn't be affected by it every time they stepped foot in an airport. They thought it was unnecessary, but to me, it was more than that. To me, I wasn't just being robbed of my time; I was being robbed of my dignity as a decent human being.

Edan Ganie

When I got upset with the officers, it wasn't simply because they had thrown a kink in my day. Yes, it was an annoyance to know that I always had to leave an hour or four earlier than anyone else because it was likely I would be stopped somewhere along the way for additional searches and questioning, but that was the smallest of the issues at hand. I could plan ahead to be sure that I made flights, but what I couldn't do was change the looks on the people's faces who watched as I was escorted off planes and held at Immigration.

I couldn't make the officers who were questioning me stop to realize that they weren't talking to a killer, but a father of three, a husband, a brother, a child of ill parents—a man. Just a man. Not a terrorist or a cold-blooded killer, but a peaceful Muslim man who loves his God, his faith, his family, and his new homeland and just wants to be successful enough that his parents could finally rest after years of hardship.

Some of the men and women who pulled me aside were understanding, like the Japanese-American officer whose grandparents had been treated the same way after Pearl Harbor and the officers in Guyana who apologized to me for having to take up my time with pointless interviews, but there have also been, and continue to be, plenty who see me as guilty until proven innocent. They pull me in and they run with the assumption that I've done something to deserve this— that *their* country would be safer without me in it.

I know by the hateful comments and the suggestive questions that some of the individuals who have sat me down to interrogate me assume that all Muslims

How I Became a Terrorist

are bad, and that we are all a threat. They don't care if their beliefs are a form of prejudice, racism or hate; they only know that it was a handful of Muslims who executed 9-11, so Muslims are something to be scared of and to hate. What they don't know is that the Muslim community has suffered immeasurably from those unfathomable attacks. Not only were innocent Muslims killed in the attacks as well, but since that day Muslims all over the United States have had to walk in fear of the judgment of others.

CHAPTER SIXTEEN:

Terrorist, Terrorist supporter, or terrorist sympathizer

> You have been subject to an inspection for a variety of reasons, some of which include your travel documents are incomplete or you do not have the proper documents or visa; you have previously violated one of the laws of CBP enforces; you have a name that matches a person of interest in one of the government's enforcements database; or you have been selected for a random search.

I was given a sheet of paper with these words in an attempt to explain to me CBP's policy in response to my inquiry as to why I am often met at the door of a plane by two CBP officers and taken in for four hours of questioning. It's been over one decade since the World Trade Center was destroyed by Middle Eastern terrorists, and since then young men have been shipped off to Guantanamo Bay and other unknown destinations. I can't help but wonder why our government officials can still not protect our borders without continuously harassing innocent law-abiding citizens like myself.

Edan Ganie

Time and time I have been questioned and asked to provide my travel documents proving my identity. Time and time again I have cooperated with the authorities and have been cleared. What is so amusing is that these incidents continue to repeat themselves; I have been stopped dozens of times in two years. I continue to seek the help of our highest level of government officials to bring resolution to this issue, but it seems that our elected leaders are powerless in protecting our nation's citizens, or they simply have no concerns for the rights of Muslim citizens.

Over the years, through the efforts of my attorney, I have appealed to various leaders responsible for national security for help. We provide all related documents showing my identity and declare my innocence relating to whatever suspicions may linger, but to no avail.

One of my earliest attempts in May 2011 was correspondence to CBP trying to clear any erroneous information they may have about me that causes me to be singled out for interrogations and searches. On July 21, 2011, I received a response from CBP, a letter signed by a compliant officer. The letter directed me to submit a request for "redress" to Department of Homeland Security Traveler Redress Inquiry Program (TRIP). It claimed that people who have been repeatedly identified for additional screening could file an inquiry to have erroneous information corrected and that TRIP was the single point of contact for individuals who have inquiries to seek resolution regarding difficulties they experience during their travels. I immediately

How I Became a Terrorist

filed a request with TRIP for redress and provided all required documents.

On August 16, 2011, I received a response from the director of DHS TRIP. She stated that DHS received my application and issued me a redress control number to provide to airlines when I made reservations. The redress number would supposedly "assist security technologies to help prevent misidentifications from occurring..." I have since used the redress number when I travel but it has done nothing to cease the screenings and interrogations. I still continue to be selected for secondary screenings and searches. As a matter of fact, it seems that the secondary screenings have since intensified.

About one year after receiving the redress number, I have experienced five more embarrassing moments in which CBP officers meet me at the airport ramps and take me for interrogations. Because of this, I sought the aid of Council on American-Islamic Relations. The reason I looked to CAIR was that I saw the ugly trend of Muslims being selected for these secondary screenings while being detained at our nation's border crossings.

The Civil Rights coordinator of CAIR – Washington Chapter wrote a letter to Secretary Janet Napolitano, US Department of Homeland Security, requesting a copy of my file from Homeland Security, Customs and Border Patrol, citing the Freedom of Information Act, seeking all records maintained by CBP.

On March 27, 2012, Dorothy Pullo, Director of FOIA Division of CBP, responded to the Council on American-Islamic Relations letter stating that they

Edan Ganie

produced 57 pages as a response to our FOIA request. The letter went on to state that 57 pages were partially releasable pursuant to information that would be detrimental to the security of transportation if released.

We carefully reviewed the 57 pages of highly redacted information we received. Most of the information compiled by CBP was unreadable. However of the portions we could have read, there were several errors regarding my personal history.

On April 26, 2012, a spokesperson for CAIR Washington wrote to Secretary Janet Napolitano and highlighted the factual errors contained in my personal files.

Some are as follows:

- Report of May 7, 2011 stopped by Agent Chako;
- Report of July 20, 2011 stopped at Peach Arch Port of Entry;
- Report of September 27, 2011 stopped at George Bush International Airport.

We pointed out to Secretary Napolitano that given the large portions or redacted data that we had no access to and the limited information we could access from the 57 pages, we started to reason that more significant factual errors may exist in my file unbeknownst to me. We further asked that the errors we found be corrected and that we be provided a clean copy of my file to certify that no other errors exist.

April 26, 2012

Secretary Janet Napolitano
U.S. Department of Homeland Security
Washington, DC 20528

Via U.S. Mail and Facsimile: 202.612.1976

**Re: Inappropriate secondary screening of Mr.
Edan Ganie, Passport No. ——**

Dear Secretary Napolitano:

I hope this letter reaches you in the best of
health and spirits. I am writing you regarding
the ongoing delays experienced by Mr. Edan
Ganie when traveling on business trips due to
interrogation and searches conducted by CBP
officers. As is routinely suggested for all travelers
experiencing repeated delays for secondary
screening, Mr. Ganie filed a TRIP request and
received his redress number, #——. Despite
Mr. Ganie pursuing resolution through the
recommended avenues, he is still experiencing
problems when traveling internationally for
work despite his status as a U.S. citizen. Mr.
Sadique has authorized the Washington State
chapter of the Council on American-Islamic
Relations (CAIR-WA) to contact you on his
behalf in a signed statement enclosed with this
letter.

On August 16, 2011, we filed a FOIA
request with CBP regarding the reason and
details of Mr. Ganie's numerous stops. On
March 27, 2012, we received 57 partially
redacted pages pertaining to Mr. Ganie's long

Edan Ganie

international travel history. While reviewing these documents, we were surprised to find factual errors regarding Mr. Ganie's personal history. The errors are detailed as follows:

- **Report of May 7, 2011 stop by CBP agent Chako**

  Notes from the interview with Mr. Ganie stated that Mr. Ganie served in the Guyanese military for two years prior to immigrating to the United States. Mr. Ganie states that this is not true, nor did he indicate such to a CBP officer. Mr. Ganie stated that his brother, who served in the US military, infantry division, sponsored him which took two years. Mr Ganie was responding to Mr. Chako's question how Mr. Ganie arrived in the US.

  The interview notes stated, "The subject stated he was a practicing Sunni Muslim." However, the interview notes fail to indicate that Mr. Ganie was questioned at length about his religious and political beliefs. Mr. Ganie was questioned about his political beliefs and asked if he would be willing to die for his country. Mr. Chako allegedly stated that if Mr. Ganie was not willing to die for his country, he shouldn't be in the United States. Further, Mr. Chako questioned Mr. Ganie about his religion, including whether he was a Sunni or Shi'ite Muslim. Mr. Chako's notes read as though Mr. Ganie offered this information voluntarily, which he did not.

How I Became a Terrorist

Interview notes indicated that Mr. Ganie stated that he "transferred to Pierce College where he obtained a bachelors degree." Mr. Ganie transferred from Pierce College to Evergreen State College where he obtained his bachelors degree.

Interview notes also contained information about Mr. Ganie's company, Edan Global Investment Management, Inc. The interview notes stated that "the company was trading company that sells cell phones to one individual in Guyana." Mr. Ganie says this is incorrect. Mr. Ganie says he told Mr. Chako that Edan Global Investment, Inc. is his management company that contracts with my other companies. Mr. Ganie further stated that Exeim Imports (a Guyanese company) imports cell phones to Guyana.

The interview notes contained incorrect information about Mr. Ganie's registration of his companies in Nevada as well. The interview stated that Mr. Ganie's companies are located in Nevada "because he could shelter his taxes that way." Mr. Ganie states this is incorrect. Mr. Ganie explained to Mr. Chako that the reason for having registered these companies in Nevada was because of legal and accounting advice relating to tax advantage and limited liabilities protection.

Interview notes were also incorrect regarding Mr. Ganie's income. Mr. Ganie explained to Mr. Chako that his base salary is $—— and then this would have to

Edan Ganie

include the reported income from several schedule Ks from the various companies where he partners. This information was not reflected accurately in the interview notes about Mr. Ganie's sources of income.

Nearly a full page of interview notes are redacted from these records.

- **Report of July 30, 2011 stop at Peach Arch Port of Entry**
  The interview notes indicated that Mr. Ganie was returning to the United States from Canada after attending his nephew's wedding. Mr. Ganie states that this information is not true, nor did he such to a CBP officer. Mr. Ganie's nephew has been married for approximately twelve years.

  Though roughly half of the interview notes were redacted, the notes indicated that Mr. Ganie was held for near five hours, from 1928 to 0010 hours.

- **Report of September 29, 2011 stop at George Bush Intercontinental Aiport**
  The interview notes indicated that Mr. Ganie was returning from a trip to Guyana where he "met with his lawyer...who is a business partner for his import business. Mr. Ganie states that this is not true, nor did he indicate such to a CBP officer. Mr. Ganie's lawyer is not a business partner.

Provided the factual errors about Mr. Ganie's history and travels throughout the documents provided by CBP and the large sections of

How I Became a Terrorist

redacted content from the interviews with Mr. Ganie, it stands to reason that other, more significant factual errors may exist in Mr. Ganie's file which are unbeknownst to him. Mr. Ganie has no criminal history and is a U.S. citizen. The excessive and consistent secondary searches to which Mr. Ganie has been subjected restrict him from the full benefits and privileges of American citizenship. Mr. Ganie, like many other American Muslims, is afforded fewer of the privileges of American citizenship than other citizens who are permitted to travel freely.

We request that the Department of Homeland Security immediately clarify the reason for Mr. Ganie's repeated delays at the border despite his status as a law-abiding American citizen. Further, we request that DHS correct any errors in the CBP system or database which does not recognize TRIP requests and if such an endeavor cannot be completed immediately, a timeline of its anticipated completion.

I look forward to speaking with you soon and discussing the problems laid forth in this letter. I can be reached via email at civilrights@wa.cair.com or via phone at 206.367.4081

Sincerely,

Jennifer Gist
Civil Rights Coordinator

Enclosure: Signed Information Release Statement
Cc: Honorable Maria Cantwell, United States Senate

Edan Ganie

Honorable Patty Murray, United States Senate
Honorable Rick Larsen, House of Representatives, 2nd Congressional District
Honorable Chris Gregoire, Governor
Chief Marco Lopez, Chief of Staff, Customs and Border Protection
Mr. Alan Bersin, Commissioner, Customs and Border Protection
Mr. David V. Aguilar, Deputy Commissioner, Customs and Border Protection
Ms. Michele James, CBP Director of Field Operations
Mr. Greg Alvarez, Area Port Director
Ms. Margo Schlanger, Officer for Civil Rights and Civil Liberties, DHS
Mr. Kareem Shora, Office for Civil Rights and Civil Liberties, DHS
Mr. Brett Laduzinsky, Office of the Commissioner, Customs and Border Protection
Mr. Arsalan Bukhari, Executive Director, CAIR-Washington
Mr. Edan Ganie

To date we have not received a response from Secretary Janet Napolitano.

Over the span of several months, I had several phone discussions and email conversations with Senator Maria Cartwell's office. After months of my attorney filing for a redress number, and then providing the number to the staff member dealing with my CBP complaint, I was asked to fill out a form granting the

How I Became a Terrorist

senator request of information from my file with CBP. So on June 28, 2011, I provided the senator's office with all the information needed to access my files. I also submitted the following letter:

July 11, 2012

Senator Maria Cantwell
915 Second Avenue, Suite 3206
Seattle, Washington 98174

Dear Senator Cantwell:

I am writing you regarding the ongoing secondary screening and interrogation by Custom and Border Patrol (CBP) when I travel for business, as well as personal trips with my family. Stephen Yim of your office has been kind in helping with my current CBP travel issues. Can you kindly provide me with copies of all correspondences and or letters written by your office on my behalf and responses received to date?

I migrated to the United States legally in 1978 and became a naturalized US citizen since 1984 (Passport No. ——). I have resided in Washington continuously and have no criminal record. Last year, I filed a TRIP request and received a redress number (——). Unfortunately, I still continue to experience the secondary screenings and interrogations every time I travel. In addition, I am listed by CBP as *"quad S"* meaning that the moment of purchasing an airline ticket I am selected for secondary screening. THIS IS NOT

Edan Ganie

RANDOM. **What is of more concern is that every single time I travel internationally and reenter the US, two CBP officers will meet me at the door of the plane and escort me to a secure area for questions and interrogations.** This is very embarrassing to me in front of my business colleagues and associates, not to say the least that it is done in front of hundreds of travelers who look at me in contemptuous ways. I have experienced such embarrassments eight times within the past 18 months. I am concern that CBP may have inaccurate and erroneous information about me that is leading to these secondary screenings, interrogations and extensive delays at the borders.

I pray that someday I will be given the opportunity to travel as all American Citizens do without being profiled, secondarily searched and interrogated.

Sincerely,

Edan Ganie, MBA
President/CEO

During follow-up phone conversations and emails with the staff member, I shared my many CBP encounters. For weeks after our phone call, I heard nothing from the senator's office. I was persistent though and followed up with emails, but still I was getting nowhere. I finally called the senator's office and asked the operator if he the staff member I had been in contact with was in.

"Yes, sir," she told me. "He is."

How I Became a Terrorist

"My name is Edan Ganie and he is handling a complaint I have concerning CBP and I would like to speak with him," I explained.

"He is on a phone call right now, Mr. Ganie," the woman said. "Can I take a message for him?"

"No thank you," I told her, trying not to sound agitated. "I will wait on the line until he can speak to me."

"I can take a message and have him call you back, sir," she pushed. "I have no way to tell how long he may be on the phone."

"I will wait," I insisted. I knew if I didn't I may never hear from him.

"Okay then," she gave in. "Please hold and I will connect you when his line is open."

"Thank you," I said, and waited for several minutes until I finally heard the voice of the elusive staff member I had been trying to contact for so long.

"This is Edan Ganie," I said when he answered. "I have been trying to contact you about my complaint."

"Hello, Mr. Ganie," he said, his words were hurried. "I apologize for that, but the reason I haven't been responsive is that there is nothing more that we can do for your complaint."

I was shocked when I heard this. I sat stunned for a moment, and then asked, "So what can I do to get this rectified and get my name off these lists?"

"The only suggestion that I have for you is to sue the government."

I could not believe that the senator's aide had just suggested suing the US government as a solution to

149

Edan Ganie

my problem with CBP. Needless to say, I was less than pleased with the proposed resolution and with the way in which I had been dealt, so the conversation ended shortly thereafter.

That was not the last time I heard from the senator's office, however. On September 16, 2012, I received a letter from Senator Cartwell's office in response to my request to receive copies of all the information the senator's office had regarding me. Instead of providing the information, the latter stated that the senator appreciated that I brought the matter to their attention and how they were happy that I gave them the opportunity to help me. Attached to the letter was an August 23, 2012, letter from Michael J. Yeager, Assistant Commissioner, US Customs and Border Patrol.

The letter from CBP to Senator Cartwell was similar to a letter I received from CBP a year earlier when I sent my initial inquiries and was directed to the Department of Homeland Security (DHS) Travel Redress Inquiry Program (TRIP); it contained the same paragraphs with the same language. Because I had already been in contact with TRIP and had been issued a number, which had not stopped the screening or profiling, I knew that the letter I just received was merely the senator's attempt at passing the buck, so to speak.

I also enlisted the help of Congressman Adam Smith's office regarding the constant and humiliating secondary screenings. The woman I worked with was compassionate and genuinely tried to help me. She was particularly concerned about the incident at the Blaine

How I Became a Terrorist

border in which my children and I were detained for five and half hours without anything to eat and nowhere to sit. Although she seemed sincere in her attempts to help, she sent a letter on October 29, 2012, stating that she spoke with a customs officer at CBP in Washington DC and that based on the information the officer found in the database, the CBP could do no more than refer me to TRIP; yet another dead-end.

The email further went on to inform me that the CBP could not share with Congressman Adam's office what, if anything, is in my file that may be causing the continued special treatment I receive at the borders. In addition, any further inquiries would not change the information CBP uses to make their decision during my border crossings. Therefore, based on the CBP response and referral, the CBP officer must close further inquiry into my database file.

Even though I received one discouraging letter after the next, I continued my pursuits to seek a resolution to the prejudiced secondary screenings. On August 15, 2012, I even wrote to President Barrack Obama and explained the difficulties I encounter when I travel. The following is the letter I sent:

August 15, 2012

The Honorable President Barak Obama
The White House
1600 Pennsylvania Avenue, NW
Washington, DC 20500

**RE:Continuous secondary screening and
interrogation by Custom and Border**

Edan Ganie

**Protection–Passport No. —— –
Redress No. ——**

Dear Mr. President:

My name is Edan Ganie, a husband, a father of two sons in college and a teenage daughter in grade school I legally migrated as a teenager from Guyana to the United States in 1978 and became a naturalized United States citizen since 1984. I am a 53 years old law-abiding citizen with no criminal record. I am a small business owner with scores of employees and have resided continuously in Washington for 34 years with outstanding contributions to my community.

I am writing you regarding the ongoing secondary screenings and interrogations by Custom and Border Patrol (CBP) when I travel for business, as well as personal trips with my family. I travelled extensively over the years to several international and nationwide destinations for business, and on occasions, I have traveled with one way tickets as necessitated by my business needs. However, about two years ago, I noticed that CBP began selecting me, every time I travelled, for secondary screenings and searches of my bags, briefcase, wallet, cellular phone and other personal and business items. Last year, I filed a "TRIP request" and received a "redress" number ——. Unfortunately, I still continue to experience the secondary screenings, interrogations and harassments.

What is of utmost concern is that every single time I travel internationally and

How I Became a Terrorist

reenter the US two CBP officers will meet me at the door of the plane and escort me to a secure area for questions and interrogations. All of my flights boarding pass will have "SSSS" printed on them, meaning that I have been selected for secondary screening. **THIS IS NOT RANDOM**. It is very embarrassing to me in front of my business colleagues and associates, not to say the least that it is done in front of hundreds of travelers who look at me in contemptuous ways. I have experienced such embarrassments eight times within the past 18 months (See attached list of travels). These extensive delays by CBP have caused financial harm to my businesses as well as emotional stress to me and love ones.

I have written to the US Customs and Border Protection Agency on several occasions without any success of learning why they continue to select me for secondary screening and interrogations. CBP provided me with documents of my travels, unfortunately, large portions are redacted. In review of the readable portions of the documents and found several errors and inaccuracies and written to Secretary Janet Napolitano asking to correct them. I also solicited the help of the Honorable Senator Maria Cantwell's staff seeking to clarify and resolve the issues that CBP may have about me. Unfortunately, to date, neither CBP nor Homeland Security have provided us with any information why I am being detained, searched, interrogated and harassed at the airport and US borders. I am concern that CBP may have

153

Edan Ganie

inaccurate and erroneous information about me that is leading to these secondary screenings, interrogations and extensive delays at the borders.

I humbly ask for your help to immediately clarify the reasons why I am being repeatedly and continuously experiencing such harassment of two CBP officers meeting me at the plane with delays of three to four hours of interrogations and searches of my personal items. I further plea for your assistance in resolving the aforementioned issues and that I am cleared of any secondary search list that I may be on. I continue to pray that someday I will be given the opportunity to travel as all American Citizens do without being profiled, secondarily searched, interrogated and harassed.

Thank you Mr. President for your time and attention to the problems herein stated. I look forward to hearing from you soon. I can be reached at —— or —— or by email at ——.

Sincerely,
Edan Ganie, MBA
President/CEO

Enclosure:List of Travels Encountering CBP Secondary Searches and Interrogations.

Cc: Honorable Maria Cantwell, United States Senate
Honorable Janet Napolitano, Secretary US Department of Homeland Security
Jennifer Gist, Civil Rights Coordinator, CAIR Washington

How I Became a Terrorist

Matt Lauer, Host, The Today Show – NBC
Morley Safer, Reporter, 60 Minutes – CBS

I received a response on October 31, 2012, from John P. Wagner, Executive Director, Admissibility and Passenger Program, Customs and Border Protection, which contained the same standard canned paragraphs that the previous letters had, explaining that "CBP is tasked with protecting the nation's border…," but failing to address the problem a hand.

I have pursued the help of seven government agencies, including Homeland Security; Customs and Border Protection; Transportation Security Administration; as well as my elected senator and congressman. Moreover, I wrote to the president of the United States soliciting help. The only thing I have learned from all my inquiries and pleas is that I am not authorized to know the information in my own file. The respective government agencies refuse to be transparent with me regarding the issue.

The only time I did receive a copy of my files from CBP, most of the materials were redacted. In reviewing the file that had not been heavily altered and cut into pieces, I found several errors concerning my personal information, and those erroneous facts have been entered into my file and are used by government agencies to stop and interview me time and time again. If I was able to find so many errors in the bit of information I was provided, I cannot help but wonder what other misinformation lays within those files, which is likely the root to all my travelling problems.

Edan Ganie

I have taken every avenue I could imagine in an attempt to put an end to the harassment I face each time I travel. From my congressman all the way up to the president, I have contacted officials seeking some kind of help with this. Unfortunately all of my elected leaders have been ineffectual at best. The only answer I have been given thus far as to the reason for the never-ending badgering and interrogations is that I must be stopped and questioned to be sure that I have not come into contact with a terrorist, a terrorist supporter, or a terrorist sympathizer during my travels. The searches, the questioning, the pat-downs and hostility—all of this is done because I may have come into contact with a person either involved or loosely associated with a terrorist organization. The question is, how would I even know if I had?

CHAPTER SEVENTEEN:

Are You a Terrorist?

On December 18, 2012, I was at work in my office engaged in a conference call with my two brothers and some business associates on the east coast. My cell phone rang during the call. I glanced at the screen to see who it was. The number was unrecognizable, so I told my brothers and colleagues that I would need to take the call.

I was surprised to find out that the anonymous number was coming from a CBP officer. The man calling identified himself as Officer Grants, a senior special agent for CBP, more specifically a field agent tasked with clearing up matters concerning my travel difficulties. He asked if he could meet with me in my office. I was somewhat hesitant at first, but after speaking with my brothers I agreed to a meeting.

"I'm in Olympia," he told me. "That isn't far from you so I can be there fairly quickly. I'll be coming with a colleague."

About an hour later Grants and his associate, who identified himself as Keith O'Brien of the FBI, arrived at my office. My assistant brought them into my office where I was still on a conference call. I excused myself

Edan Ganie

from the call and took the two men to the conference room. We all said hello and introduced ourselves, then I got to the point.

"What specifically do you need from me to clear up the CBP issues?" I asked Grants once we were all seated.

"If you could explain your business and reasons for travel, that would be a starting point," he replied.

I was willing to do whatever it took to be able to walk through an airport like anyone else, so I readily accepted his assignments. I stood up and began drawing a chart on the white board showing the various companies my brothers and I operate. I broke the chart into individual industries and by company for each industry. I explained the rational for the separate companies, discussing the legal independence liabilities, taxes, etc. for each company. I further showed that each company is unique in its partnership formation and it helped to keep the respective company's business separate from the others—that it makes sense for better business reporting and management. I was diligent in my explanations so there would be no room for questions.

Grants had a few more questions about my business in the Caribbean and I answered each concern he had clearly and with as much detail as possible. He wanted to know about some operational procedures and I clarified those as well. He was curious about a particular ex-employee and I explained who he was and his job title while he worked for us.

"He hasn't been with us for about two years now, though," I told them.

How I Became a Terrorist

"What is your involvement in the local Muslim community?" Grants asked next.

During the interview, my sons, who were both in their late teens, came in to do some work around the office and I introduced them to the officers. Grants made mention of how polite they both were and I told them that they were products of home schooling and Islamic schooling, which led us to the discussion concerning my ties with the Muslim community, so I explained that to him.

"Can you tell me about your religious donations?" he went on.

"I only make donations to organizations and persons I know," I answered. "I am a founding member of our Mosque and have been involved in the executive body over the years, so I make donations to the Mosque but I am fully aware of how the money is spent. My religious contributions are listed in my taxes," I added.

By the time I had gone through my involvement with the Mosque, our meeting was approaching the two-hour mark and we were about to wrap it up.

"I have one last question," Grants said as he glanced from me to O'Brien and tinkered with his pen, "but I'm not too comfortable as how to ask it."

"Just ask it outright," I told him.

"Are you a terrorist?" asked Grants.

I didn't like the question at all, but I wasn't terribly surprised by it either.

"No," was my unequivocal answer. "In no way am I a terrorist, terrorist supporter or terrorist sympathizer."

Edan Ganie

With the elephant in the room finally taken care of, I took some time to point out that the CBP had detained me over fifteen times within the past two years, each time for 3-4 hours.

"The routine seems the same and the questions seem the same," I told them. "So why do they continue to interrogate me, to embarrass and harass me, by sending two CBP officers to meet me at the plane every time? It seems like a waste of resources."

Grants did the best to answer me, but ultimately moved to his conclusion. "The reason for the meeting was to get an understanding of your business and travels," he said, redirecting the focus of the conversation. "We will clear things up but it will take some time." With that, we thanked one another and the meeting ended.

Two months later, I received a call from O'Brien. He explained that he and Grants had a few follow-up questions and would like to do one more interview so they could get everything cleared up. We agreed to meet in Tacoma at the FBI office, but Grants was not there when I arrived.

"Grants is comfortable with us doing the meeting without him," O'Brien assured me, and then he went into the questioning.

The interview wasn't exactly what I expected. Instead of asking about me, O'Brien gave some details of another man and asked if I knew this individual and if I had any information on him.

"Yes," I told him. "I know him."

"How did you all meet?"

How I Became a Terrorist

I explained how I met this particular person, and then O'Brien asked if I knew his father, which I did. Beyond that, I didn't know personal details, so our interview was a short one. I was unclear as to how this man that I vaguely knew played a role in my problems with the CBP and travelling, but was glad the interview was brief.

On the way out, O'Brien assured me that they were working on a resolution to my travel issues, but still I have seen no major change and still I am picked out for secondary screenings and stopped when I re-enter the country, and I can only assume that it is because of my ethnicity. I think Grants proved that to me when he dropped the big question, "Are you a terrorist?" during our interview. And though he asked the question, he never explained why it even needed to be asked; no one has.

The fact is, the vast majority of the Islamic nation has no affiliation with extremists and are as fearful of al Qaeda as everyone else in the world, but still we are set apart by many because of Islamophobia. Mosques have been desecrated, protests have broken out opposing the building of places of worship, and travelling has become all but unbearable for millions who wear burqas, headscarves, turbans, or even look of Middle Eastern descent, all because a minority of extremists did something unspeakable, which has caused millions of ill-informed and misguided individuals to cling to their fear and hate rather than to understand the plight of another.

Edan Ganie

In the United States, where the first pilgrims came in search for religious freedom and tolerance, it is unfortunate and shameful that there is so little freedom or tolerance for certain faiths, and that is something that must change unless we want to remain a nation of terrified hypocrites—a nation of people still fearing what they do not understand.

Epilogue

Every time I am pulled aside for secondary screening, taken off a flight to have my bag searched, held at a border for hours without explanation, or pulled out of a crowd for an "interview," I am being targeted as a terrorist, a threat, or a bad person trying to do bad things without any justification. Every time that a uniformed officer or a flight attendant approaches me and asks me to follow them, I'm not just being inconvenienced; I am being profiled and I am losing my credibility as a decent human being for crimes I never committed or never happened. These searches and interrogations are not just unfair; they are a breach of my civil rights, but no one seems to be concerned about that, and I have to wonder, why?

Why are my rights less valuable than others? Why is it okay to vilify me and probe into my personal life? What about me makes me more likely to be a terrorist supporter than any other American? Did Marines experience the same backlash because of the horrendous act that Timothy McVey executed in Oklahoma City that sorrowful day on April 19, 1995? Did every serviceman who wanted to rent a moving

Edan Ganie

truck or fertilize their lawn get pulled into a tiny concrete room to be questioned by two or three officers about why they were moving, where they were moving to, and who they were moving in with? Did officers want to know how big their yards were and how their yards were landscaped before they would let them purchase fertilizer? I think it would be safe to bet that, no, that was not a consequence of that terrorist attack; and make no mistake, Timothy McVey was a terrorist.

This nation has come to think of the words Muslim and terrorist as synonymous. If a news story comes up about a bomb threat or an incident in an airport, most people assume that there was a Muslim behind it. That has made it easy for Americans to lump all Muslims into a nasty whole—a category of malicious, barbaric people who want to destroy the West and take over the world. It has also created a sense of dread for many Muslims for fear of how we will be treated in response to these horribly inaccurate and slanderous stereotypes.

I was a child in the sixties, living in a small village in a small country in the Caribbean. Guyana gained independence from the British Imperialists in the sixties and quickly became an authoritarian ruled society in which individual citizens lost their freedom and civil liberties. Those who spoke up against the Tyrannical government were harassed, persecuted and imprisoned. As a result, the country saw a mass exodus of its citizens leaving for opportunities and freedom in countries like England, Canada and United States of America.

How I Became a Terrorist

As a child I was told that America was the land of opportunity and I dreamt of coming to America. My dreams and prayers came true when I received my residence visa in 1978 to live in America. I immediately migrated and began searching for my American dream.

I worked hard and pursued my education. I worked for small businesses, large corporations and the government. Then I took the entrepreneur risk and ventured into business. With hard work and perseverance I became successful. I am conscious of giving back to my community and do so in many ways. However, I noticed that by being a Muslim after September 11, I am not treated the way every other hard-working American is. I am profiled, harassed and interrogated by my government, all in the interest of national security, yet I am a law-abiding citizen.

Modern Muslims in America have come to embody the fright of being harassed by a government abusing civil liberties. How ironic? Mr. Obama in his State of the Union Address stated that Americans must remain a beacon for all who seek freedom. He went on to say that in the Middle East we will stand fast with all who seek liberty. I could not help but consider the hypocrisy of President Obama's speech, because here I am in the United States of America, the land of freedom and liberty, but I am profiled and harassed, my civil liberties stifled. How can he seek to liberate people halfway around the world but oppress his own outstanding citizens in America? Some example of beacon for us to share with those people in the Middle East who seek freedom and liberty.

Edan Ganie

For Muslim emigrants all over the US, especially from the Middle East, being treated as a criminal because of a gross misunderstanding and overall ignorance of their faith has become commonplace. For these people, fear and freedom have become terms frequently associated with their new homeland. Ironically, the mixture of the two is a paradoxical one. If fear prevents a people from using their voices or pens, that fear eventually destroys freedom and happiness.

I know families, friends and others who share similar experiences to mine but are afraid to speak up. From time to time, I run into some of these people and I can see that the fear that they cultivated in their minds has destroyed their freedom and their happiness. Fear of their government has stolen their unalienable rights.

I took heed to the words of our President Barack Obama in his February 12, 2013 State of the Union Address. He said that when you work hard and meet your responsibilities, you can get ahead. I agree with him. However, when you are a Muslim and become successful, things are not so clear-cut. You become a target subject to national security profiling and harassment once you've accomplished dreams and gained success.

In the world's proclaimed country of freedom, Muslims are living their lives in trepidation. It is known that the United States of America is the land of opportunity. People from all nations, near and far, dream of one day coming to this great nation to claim or find their dream. Unfortunately, in my case as an innocent Muslim who came to the United States of

How I Became a Terrorist

America and studied, worked hard, became a successful businessman, raised a family and economically, socially and morally contributes to this great land of freedom and liberty, I am profiled as a terrorist or as someone who may come into contact with a terrorist, a terrorist supporter, or a terrorist-sympathizer, simply because of my faith. It isn't my faith that is to be blamed for this though, it is Islamophobia and its acceptance.

For so long, the news pumped in images of bearded men cloaked in filthy clothes hiding out in caves and organizing attacks across the globe as the only representation of a Muslim, and it seems that the public has readily adopted that view. That acceptance has acted as a boulder that has fallen on the backs of every Muslim in the country, and it has allowed for hate and prejudice to go unchecked for far too long. It feels like the Jim Crow laws have been resurrected in a new way every time I am pulled aside and patted down. America loves to boast of its open-mindedness and how forward-thinking it is; the Statue of Liberty stands tall and proud with the inscription The New Colossus that says,

> Give me your tired, your poor,
> Your huddled masses yearning to breathe free,
> The wretched refuse of your teeming shore.
> Send these, the homeless, tempest-tost to me,
> I lift my lamp beside the golden door!"

Lady Liberty doesn't have a clause that excludes anyone for their faith or nationality, but America seems to have created one and set it firmly into place. I feel

Edan Ganie

this clause each time I'm asked to step aside. I feel it when I'm asked to give detailed descriptions of where I've been and who I've been into contact with. I feel it when I'm asked what I do for a living and how much money I make, and expected to answer if I want to get home to my family. And I really feel it when I send one letter after another to government officials, hoping to find some kind of solution, but hear no response and see no action taken place to remedy the injustice.

Decades ago Dr. King fought and died trying to erase prejudice and hate from the American landscape. This country has come a long way from the time that Dr. King was killed as far as it's black-white relations go, but we are blind if we can't see that we still have a long way to go when fighting prejudice.

This book is my contribution to the fight because if everyone stays quiet and waits for the profiling and the prejudice to pass, it may hang thick over us forever, and I want to know that when my grandchildren are adults, there will be no more protests against the building of mosques, no more senseless interrogations for those of Middle eastern descent, and it will not be okay to ask a man or woman what faith they are before they are allowed to step foot on an airplane.

I have become actively engaged in doing all I can to expose the discrimination that takes place in the country today. Like many others, I too have medical issues, but I will fight in hopes that I can somehow make a difference for the generations to come. In an attempt to find real solutions to the problems of the Muslim community, I have contacted the Council on

How I Became a Terrorist

American-Islamic Relations to help me, as well as written letters to a number of government officials explaining my problem. I have provided some of the letters that I have written to officials and I urge anyone reading this who has had similar experiences to my own to do the same. There is strength in numbers, so I plead with all of you out there who have been quiet for so long to speak up. If we all choose to break the silence, our voices will be heard.

Additional Letters to Government Officials

July 11, 2012

Senator Maria Cantwell
915 Second Avenue, Suite 3206
Seattle, Washington 98174

Dear Senator Cantwell:

I am writing you regarding the ongoing secondary screening and interrogation by Custom and Border Patrol (CBP) when I travel for business, as well as personal trips with my family. Stephen Yim of your office has been kind in helping with my current CBP travel issues. Can you kindly provide me with copies of all correspondences and or letters written by your office on my behalf and responses received to date?

I migrated to the United States legally in 1978 and became a naturalized US citizen since 1984 (Passport No. ———). I have resided in Washington continuously and have no criminal record. Last year, I filed a TRIP request and received a redress number (———).

Edan Ganie

Unfortunately, I still continue to experience the secondary screenings and interrogations every time I travel. In addition, I am listed by CBP as *"quad S"* meaning that the moment of purchasing an airline ticket I am selected for secondary screening. THIS IS NOT RANDOM. **What is of more concern is that every single time I travel internationally and reenter the US, two CBP officers will meet me at the door of the plane and escort me to a secure area for questions and interrogations.**

This is very embarrassing to me in front of my business colleagues and associates, not to say the least that it is done in front of hundreds of travelers who look at me in contemptuous ways. I have experienced such embarrassments eight times within the past 18 months. I am concern that CBP may have inaccurate and erroneous information about me that is leading to these secondary screenings, interrogations and extensive delays at the borders.

I pray that someday I will be given the opportunity to travel as all American Citizens do without being profiled, secondarily searched and interrogated.

Sincerely,

Edan Ganie, MBA
President/CEO

How I Became a Terrorist

November 6, 2012

John P. Wagner, Executive Director
US Customs and Border Patrol
Admissibility and Passenger Programs
Office of Field Operations
1300 Pennsylvania Avenue NW
Washington, DC 20219

RE: Redress No. ——
Edan Ganie -Passport No. ——

Dear Mr. Wagner:

This is in response to your October 31st, 2012 letter regarding my difficulties when I am processed through US Customs and Border Protection. You stated that, "CBP takes allegations of employee misconduct very seriously and has instituted policies pertaining to abuses of authority. Complaints of unprofessional conduct are recorded, investigated, and appropriate action is taken against CBP officers who are found to have violated policy." Thus, I would like to bring to your attention a very unprofessional experience with CBP when I recently reentered the Country at Miami airport.

On September 19th, I returned from a business trip and entered the country at Miami airport via flight BW 484 from Trinidad. I was met by two CBP officers at the airplane ramp and was escorted into a processing room at about 1:45 pm. They took my passport and gave it to the supervisor. I witnessed the supervisor who was a "heavy set" black female. I could see

173

Edan Ganie

she had the passport on her desk. About 15 minutes later, she took her bags and left with two of her colleagues. I still continued sitting there for the next two hours without any one helping me.

While I was there waiting only four other travelers were in the room to be processed and I counted about 11 CBP officers present. I overheard conversations among the CBP officers about buying houses, interest rates and refinancing. I heard them talking about vacations in Puerto Rico and the good times there. I heard conversations about walking dogs in the park and women with legs like broom stick jogging. I heard conversations about one of the CBP officer son boxing and going to tryouts, etc. I finally asked for a supervisor and was told there was none present because she left for the day.

After insisting to speak with someone in charge, I was taken to Mr. Hughton. By this time it was about 2:15 p.m. Mr. Hughton told me that he was not the supervisor in that particular section and was only passing through. He then called for two officers who came about 20 minutes later (Timothy and Cooper). These two officers were very courteous and professional in processing me. About a half hour later I was escorted out through the baggage area.

I am disappointed that the CBP staff would make me sit there for two hours without any help, especially while they were engaging in so many unproductive conversations. It is very

How I Became a Terrorist

unprofessional and disrespectful to those of us who were there in the room waiting to be processed. More importantly, I would like to know if it is necessary for me to be detained about three to four hours every time I am processed by CBP.

Thank you in advance for your attention to this complaint herein stated. I look forward to hearing from you soon. I can be reached at —— or —— or by email at ——.

Sincerely,

Edan Ganie, MBA
President/CEO

Enclosure:List of Travels Encountering CBP Secondary Searches and Interrogations.

Cc: The Honorable Maria Cantwell, United States Senate
The Honorable Adam Smith, United States Congress
The Honorable Janet Napolitano, Secretary US Department of Homeland Security
Jennifer Gist, Civil Rights Coordinator, CAIR Washington
Morley Safer, Reporter, 60 Minutes–CBS

Edan Ganie

October 16, 2012

Laura Lynch, Director
US Department of Homeland Security
DHS Travel Redress Inquiry Program
601 South 12th Street, TSA-901
Arlington, VA 20598-6901

**RE: Redress No. ——
Edan Ganie -Passport No. ——**

Dear Ms. Lynch:

I am writing pursuant to your April 26th, 2012 letter regarding the difficulties I experience when I travel. You stated that, you can neither confirm nor deny any information about me which may be within federal watchlists. However, based upon my recent travel experiences I wish to point out that I am selected every single time I travel and the fact that two CBP officers meet me at the plane ramp and escort me to a secure area for questions and interrogations, lasting three to four hours. **I would submit that this is neither occasional nor random and I am profiled within a watchlist.**

I am a law-abiding citizen with no criminal record. I am a husband, a father of two sons in college and a teenage daughter in grade school. I am a small business owner with scores of employees and have resided continuously in Washington for 34 years with outstanding contributions to my community. I legally migrated to the United States as a teenager from Guyana in 1978 when I was sponsored by my brother who was a US army infantry soldier. I later became a naturalized United States citizen since 1984.

How I Became a Terrorist

I travelled extensively over the years to several international and nationwide destinations as necessitated by my business needs. About two years ago, CBP began selecting me, every time I travel, as evidenced by the **"SSSS"** on my boarding passes, for secondary screenings and searches of my bags, briefcase, wallet, cellular phone and other personal and business items. What is of utmost concern is that every single time I reenter the nation's borders two CBP officers will meet me at the plane doorway and escort me into a secure area for questions, searches and interrogations. I have experienced such embarrassments 13 times within the past 18 months (See attached list of travels).

I always cooperate to the fullest extent with the CBP officers in their task with protecting our nation's borders. However, I am selected every time I travel for these secondary screenings. This is neither occasional nor random as it happens every single time I travel. I filed a "TRIP request" and received a "redress" number (——). Unfortunately, after receiving the redress, I still experienced the secondary screenings 22 consecutive times at airports within the United States. In addition to this, when returning home from international travels, I was embarrassed 13 times when two CBP officers waited for me at the aircraft ramp way and interrogated, searched and detained me for three to four hours each time. I certainly do not mind the occasional random selection for secondary searches as it helps CBP to detect and mitigate threats to our nation. However,

177

Edan Ganie

being profiled and put on a list to be selected every time for secondary screening and searches does seem to be extenuating and becomes burdensome after dozens of encounters.

I humbly ask for your help to immediately clarify the reasons why I am being repeatedly and continuously experiencing such harassments. I further plea for your assistance in resolving the aforementioned issues and that I am cleared of any secondary search list that I may be on. I continue to pray that someday I will be given the opportunity to travel as all American Citizens do without being profiled.

Thank you for your time and attention to the problems herein stated. I look forward to hearing from you soon. I can be reached at —— or —— or by email at ——.

Sincerely,

Edan Ganie, MBA
President/CEO

Enclosure:List of Travels Encountering CBP Secondary Searches and Interrogations.

Cc: The Honorable Maria Cantwell, United States Senate
The Honorable Adam Smith, United States Congress
The Honorable Janet Napolitano, Secretary US Department of Homeland Security
Jennifer Gist, Civil Rights Coordinator, CAIR Washington
Morley Safer, Reporter, 60 Minutes – CBS

How I Became a Terrorist

September 28, 2012

The Honorable Secretary Janet Napolitano
Department of Homeland Security
U.S. Department of Homeland Securit
Washington, D.C. 20528

RE:Continuous secondary screening and interrogation by Custom and Border Protection–Passport No. —— – Redress No. ——

Dear Secretary Janet Napolitano:

My name is Edan Ganie, a husband, a father of two sons in college and a teenage daughter in grade school I legally migrated as a teenager from Guyana to the United States in 1978 and became a naturalized United States citizen since 1984. I am a 53 years old law-abiding citizen with no criminal record. I am a small business owner with scores of employees and have resided continuously in Washington for 34 years with outstanding contributions to my community.

I am writing in response to an August 23, 2012 correspondence from Assistant Commissioner, Michael Yeager, Office of Congressional Affairs regarding the ongoing secondary screenings and interrogations by Custom and Border Patrol (CBP) when I travel for business, as well as personal trips with my family. About two years ago, I noticed that CBP began selecting me, every time I travelled, for secondary screenings and searches of my bags, briefcase, wallet, cellular phone and

Edan Ganie

other personal and business items. Last year, I filed a "TRIP request" and received a "redress" number (——). Unfortunately, I still continue to experience the secondary screenings, interrogations and harassments.

What is of utmost concern is that every single time I travel internationally and reenter the US two CBP officers will meet me at the door of the plane and escort me to a secure area for questions and interrogations. All of my flights boarding pass will have "SSSS" printed on them, meaning that I have been selected for secondary screening. THIS IS NOT RANDOM.

It is very embarrassing to me in front of my business colleagues and associates, not to say the least that it is done in front of hundreds of travelers who look at me in contemptuous ways. I have experienced such embarrassments 13 times within the past 18 months (See attached list of travels). These extensive delays by CBP have caused not only embarrassment and emotional stress to me – not to mention financial harm to my businesses.

I have written to the US Customs and Border Protection Agency on several occasions without any success of learning why they continue to select me for secondary screening and interrogations. CBP provided me with documents of my travels, unfortunately, large portions are redacted. In review of the readable portions of the documents I found several errors and inaccuracies and written to Secretary Janet Napolitano asking to correct them. I also

How I Became a Terrorist

solicited the help of the Honorable Senator Maria Cantwell's staff and the Honorable Congressman Adam Smith's staff seeking to clarify and resolve the issues that CBP may have about me. Unfortunately, to date, neither CBP nor Homeland Security have provided us with any clear information why I am being detained, searched, interrogated and harassed at the airport and US borders. I am concern that CBP may have inaccurate and erroneous information about me that is leading to these secondary screenings, interrogations and extensive delays at the borders.

I humbly ask for your help to immediately clarify the reasons why I am being repeatedly and continuously experiencing such harassment of two CBP officers meeting me at the plane with delays of three to four hours of interrogations and searches of my personal items. I further plea for your assistance in resolving the aforementioned issues and that I am cleared of any secondary search list that I may be on. I continue to pray that someday I will be given the opportunity to travel as all American Citizens do without being profiled, secondarily searched, interrogated and harassed.

Thank you for your time and attention to the problems herein stated. I look forward to hearing from you soon. I can be reached at —— or —— or by email at ——.

Sincerely,

Edan Ganie, MBA
President/CEO

Edan Ganie

Enclosure:List of Travels Encountering CBP Secondary Searches and Interrogations.

Cc: Honorable Maria Cantwell, United States Senate
The Honorable Adam Smith, Congress of the United States
Honorable Janet Napolitano, Secretary US Department of Homeland Security
Jennifer Gist, Civil Rights Coordinator, CAIR Washington